Praise for Bava's (

"Michael Urheber has written an inspiring and courageous story that chronicles a profound spiritual transformation based on synchronies occurring in his life. Once I started reading it, I couldn't put it down."
— Neal Grossman, author of *The Spirit of Spinoza*

"*Bava's Gift* reverberates with powerful and meaningful insight as it weaves together everyday aspects of life. It is a gift you give yourself; like miracles, a function of your perspective and love. Be prepared to be inspired, filled with hope, wonder and peace, and know that you may be lovingly guided, even in the most challenging moments of your life."
— Susan Barbara Apollon, psychologist and author of *Touched by the Extraordinary*

"*Bava's Gift* reads like a suspense novel, with dark secrets, exploring the mysteries of the Big Questions that arise after a death—mysteries of the mind that define who we are, and how we're connected. Enlightening!"
— Henry Chang, author of *Chinatown Beat*

Bava's Gift

Awakening to the Impossible

Michael Urheber

ICRL Press
Princeton, New Jersey

BAVA'S GIFT
By Michael Urheber
Copyright © 2014 by Michael Urheber

ISBN: 978-1-936033-10-2

Cover image © Michael Urheber

For information address:
ICRL Press
211 N. Harrison St., Suite C
Princeton, NJ 08540-3530

This book is dedicated to Frank Bava,
a gentle soul who taught me the game of marbles.

PRÉCIS

...the source of your arts' course springs from experiment
— Dante, *The Divine Comedy*

One of the few things my friend Frank Bava embraced about this world was the idea that he was Italian. So the discovery that he wasn't came as a shock. And by the time his mother, Evelyn, revealed the news, it was too late for Frank to reset his cultural identity. Not that he would, if given a choice. Or that anyone could, once that perception takes root in whatever part of the brain it is that prefers spaghetti *aglio e olio* rather than fried chicken or stuffed cabbage. Nevertheless, as someone willing to accept stark realities, this admission from Frank's mother coming late in Frank's teens clarified some important things about his past.

As it turned out, Frank's biological father's last name was Howard. Frank never spoke to me about him other than to say he was a drunkard, and that he occasionally spotted him roaming the neighborhood where Frank grew up and lived most of his life—Astoria, Queens. When it came to his namesake, his stepfather, Frank was equally sparing with details, sharing only one memory: "We went to a park when I was a kid. We spent about two minutes together. Then he walked off and I never saw him again."

It's fair to say that Frank and I had a mutual contempt for the paternal influences in our lives, and for that matter, family life in general. When Pavlov, the famous Russian physiologist, stopped feeding his lab dogs at the sound of the bell, their anticipation turned to disappointment. Their pre-salivating days were over. The annihilation of expectations is the other side of the famous experiment you don't often hear about. Still, you don't have to be a lab dog to know that a steady diet of abuse can breed a lifetime of contempt.

There was, of course, more to our friendship than a mistrust of paternal figures and the unstated recognition that the best way to get through life was to lower one's expectations, or simply eliminate them. While the people Frank and I needed growing up were incapable of extending love and recognition, our friendship filled a void. But what ultimately emerged from our association was more than fond memories. A simple yet unplanned experiment—not the kind that will win you a fellowship at the Sorbonne—sparked an uncanny sequence of events, and despite its whimsical start has reverberated with a persuasive force that continues to touch many people.

These events, all bordering on the miraculous, imparted here with as much veracity as any witness may dare claim, had an enormous influence on my life as I struggled to make sense of them. Because, despite such commonly accepted truths that take root in whatever part of our brain it is that is content with easy answers in a world of immense possibilities, I could no longer dismiss as mere "coincidence" the reality that was unfolding. I felt the need to understand it. To explore it. To make peace with it. And I was willing to do whatever that took.

Today, when it comes to the delicate interactions among minds and souls and things, I am no longer sure where one ends and the other begins. It is a landscape of nettles and paradox, where faith collides with reason, and no one who enters leaves the same. If you leave unchanged, it could be because you weren't listening. In my case, Frank was so insistent, I couldn't shut my ears.

Author's Note: This is a true story. I have changed the names of some individuals to protect their privacy.

CHAPTER 1

You say good-bye and I say hello. Hello. Hello.
— The Beatles

In the flow that was Frank's life, Friday, August 9, 2003, was a day that began like most others. At around 10:30 AM, he took the "F" Train from Astoria and changed at Penn Station for the "C" with a stop on Spring Street in SoHo, New York, just one block from *Anonymous*, the salon where he worked as a stylist.

Before walking through the door, he would wave to Alisandro, the owner of a small Italian deli next to the salon, check the flowers in the large window box he built himself, then pause before entering, taking a deep breath to prepare for one of his signature greetings.

"Bongiorno!" he would exclaim, clearing a big

friendly space for himself into which he would unload his bag, set up the tools of his trade, and get ready for whatever clients he had that day.

It didn't matter to Frank that Anya and Yvonne, two of his co-workers, as well as Paula, the owner of the salon, were already a few hours into their workday while he was just beginning his. At fifty-seven years of age, Frank had enough of hairdressing and was considering other employment. Paula tolerated Frank's waning schedule because they had been friends for years.

As Paula recalls, that Friday seemed typical in every respect, even Frank's morning "train story" that he shared as he coaxed from his bag a thermos of vegetable soup which he would replenish from a kiosk uptown before changing trains.

What was the "train story"?

It was the continuing saga of man's inhumanity to man, of mother's insensitivity to child, of the willful unconsciousness of strangers. In other words, the average trip on a New York City subway. Nothing inspired Frank's lyricism, a quality enriched by his Italian affinity, as much as his disdain for certain kinds of conduct. Events such as these—a mother who pointed the stroller the other way instead of consoling her sobbing child, or a teenager who refused to give up his seat for an elderly passenger—or any such lapse in kindness exhibited by a fellow traveler, would inevitably launch a tirade.

"Frank, calm down," I would say near the five-minute mark, usually about halfway through his speech.

"Okay, Michael," he'd reply. But I knew his

rhapsody wasn't complete until I heard his standard close: his desire to be transported far, far away, to a secluded cave in a remote forest, where, like an Arhat in a Chinese wood-block print, he would live peacefully, in perfect harmony with nature.

Though not nearly as idyllic, one of Frank's favorite escapes was an hour and a half away from Queens, to my house in Bucks County, Pennsylvania. That Friday, Frank called and asked if he could visit over the weekend with Jean, a friend of his.

My mother, Rose, was the one who introduced me to Frank. Neither before, nor since, had she shown any desire to introduce me to anyone in her life. Sure, I needed a haircut, but why Frank? And on that day I would never have guessed that our meeting would constitute such a pivotal link in a causal chain (I am including my actual birth in this sequence) that weighed so heavily on my being.

Usually I visited the local barber who just hacked away. But on this occasion my mother was determined to have someone more skilled cut my hair. Looking back, I realized if I looked less straggly, less like a waif, people might be less likely to notice the sense of despair enveloping my frame, and therefore less inclined to question why that was. It was an evasive maneuver, a new stitch in her cover-up. At least in hindsight that is what I think my mother had in mind. She excelled at making our shadowy world look bright. That was her talent—shielding not her child, but rather the sexual predator under our roof.

The predator was my father, a black hole in my universe. A dark energy against a dark sky that twisted life's delicate fabric around him. Let me get this piece of my own painful familial history out of the way so that I will not dwell on it any more than necessary. It will give you some idea of the ground from which I was raised, and the blessings that allow us to raise ourselves.

My father, that "paternal influence" I referenced at the start, was a brutal man. The mere expectation of his presence triggered in me an instinctual need to run and hide, like a monkey sensing a lion or snake in the vicinity and scrambling to the top of the jungle canopy for safety. Hiding spaces were my secret refuge: inside a hall closet on the highest shelf, under an end table at the intersection of two sofas, under my bed. These were places where the hungry wolf was too big to enter.

There was an action-adventure TV hero in the 1980's named MacGyver who had a gift for modifying found objects in life-death situations. For me this instinct manifested early. When I was around two years old and summarily dropped in a crib, trapped with an impending sense of doom that only a calf bound for slaughter or a condemned prisoner might know, I conceived a plan: pull myself up by the rails, reach a standing position, and shake the crib as hard as I could to move it over to the door where it would lodge, barring my father from entry. Maybe I could keep him out forever?

I succeeded, to a certain extent. There was pounding at the door. I heard shouting on the other side. But in that room, for a brief moment, I felt safe. And, for the first time, a sense of self-reliance, the idea that I could gain some control over my fate. God had given me the tools to survive, though, I will admit, it took me decades to get over my anger at Him for making things so unpleasant.

So my father had established himself with unlimited and ungodly authority, collapsing any opportunity for a secure and nurturing home that every child needs in order to decipher who or what they are. In this, unfortunately, my mother was complicit. She proved an excellent accomplice for my father who afforded her the means to sweep his vile crimes under a rug, and place fresh-cut flowers in a crystal vase.

My mother perfected this cover-up over many long years of practice. While rancor flowed beneath our feet, it never entered the visual spectrum where I hoped someone like a family friend or relative might detect what was going on and carry me to safer ground. As a child it was always a mystery to me why they hadn't. Couldn't anyone tell all was not right in Arcadia? Wasn't it obvious the Shepherd was raping the flock?

No one seemed to notice. That's how good my mother was at her appointed task. To some extent, it is also a reflection of how well I could hold up under defiling shame and humiliation—the cross that every survivor bears. Ultimately, my father was tried in absentia, because by the time I was able to confront him with his legacy of abuse, he'd been dead a few years. My mother, who was spending her last years in an assisted living facility, rejected the opportunity for truth and reconciliation and instead attempted suicide, not once, but three times. With that I abandoned my Tribunal. "In wrath, remember mercy," the prophet Habakkuk implores us.

So thanks to my mother, Frank cut my hair. Frank

was eight years my senior and because of our age difference more like a big brother at the time. We lost touch
while I was away at college. But a number of years later
when I began working in New York we bumped into
each other. I needed a haircut and ducked into a small
salon in lower Manhattan. Frank was sitting quietly,
reading a newspaper.

"Frank?" I shouted in surprise.

"Heeeeeeey Pal!" he answered back.

It was a happy moment. From then on we stayed
in touch.

For Frank, trimming hair was better than getting
his hands ripped up doing body and fender work. War-
ren Beatty's film *Shampoo* provided some inspiration
for his career change when he realized working in a
salon would be a great place to meet women. So after
seven years of restoring cars, he literally swapped an
airbrush for a hairbrush. And since he wasn't gay, he
figured the field would be wide open.

Frank's call to me that Friday was surprising for
a couple of reasons. First, menacing forecasts like rain
and cold kept him away, cloistered in Astoria, and rain
was forecast all weekend. Second, Frank had known
Jean for over fifteen years. We hadn't met in all that
time. But, for some reason, Frank wanted to introduce
us *that* weekend.

Saturday, August 10, 2003, Frank and Jean
arrived from New York on a morning train.

"Hey pal," Frank exclaimed, beaming one of his
broad grins as they walked up to my car.

"Hi Michael, I'm Jean," her voice broke in with an
arm stretched out. Jean seemed like a no-nonsense kind

of person, cordial and straightforward, and no doubt wondering herself why Frank had induced her to make the trip all the way from her brownstone in Brooklyn on an overcast weekend.

Frank's "train story" was already in motion by the time we sat down in my car. New Jersey Transit wasn't about to get a free ride. I listened as Frank denounced loud public cell-phone conversations, which for him had become the latest violation of civilized behavior. But when he reached the finish, the part in which he yearns for deeper, private communion with the natural world, the sense of wistfulness was gone. In its place was a decisive plan.

In the next few months, Frank planned to take himself off the grid and leave urban life behind. First on his agenda was a hike along the entire Appalachian Trail, from Georgia to Maine. He had it all worked out: the provisions he needed, where he would stop to take a shower and post mail, and where, if anyone wanted, they could meet up with him and hike along for a stretch.

Frank's mother had died a few months earlier. His role as caregiver was over. In his mind he had fulfilled both a filial and karmic obligation. Now there was nothing stopping him from doing what he wanted.

I was thrilled for Frank when he told me his plans. He was writing a new story for his life, and starting to live it, too. He would sell his house, give away what he no longer needed, and place in storage the few things of importance to him. With the savings he had, and money from the sale of the house, he figured he would get along fine.

Act II is where most plays, and lives, fall apart. The hero with great promise and mighty intentions loses his nerve. He can't find a way out of his predicament. One day a letter comes in the mail. It's an invitation from AARP. He accepts it. Although he never slew the dragon or found the Holy Grail, at least he can get discounts at the movies and lower rates on car insurance.

Frank had bigger plans. He stepped up his regular exercise in pursuit of his journey, which he planned to start in early March. An expert at Tai Chi, Frank also liked lifting weights and added swimming to his workout. He kept detailed records to monitor his progress. Later, his sister found some of these notes and told me he was up to thirty-five laps a day in the Astoria pool. At 330 feet, it is the largest public pool in New York. Frank was swimming over two miles a day.

I loosely connected Frank's desire to introduce Jean with his recent announcement that he was making a major course correction in his life. Still, I thought, why the urgency? It was the question occupying my mind since Frank's call the day before. Why, after fifteen years of knowing her, did he feel this was the right time for us to meet? Jean and I beheld each other with the same curiosity. Frank was directing the show and so determined to make it happen, he didn't seem to notice Jean and me stumbling on the stage. He never gave us the script. All we could do was improvise.

The weather was overcast as we left the train station. With nothing special planned, I headed back to my house through Hopewell, New Jersey, still horse-country for bluebloods like Jackie O, and the site of the kidnapping of Charles Lindbergh's baby in 1932.

We grabbed some breakfast at a local café and milled around an antique store. Following that we made a quick stop to pick up a few food items for the grill. By the time we arrived at my house, the weather had taken a turn for the better.

I live on the site of an old chicken farm that now lies nestled between a number of ready-made mansions and a few lovely historic homes. It still hints at a time when people owned less and did more, when they spent more time getting things right, instead of just getting them done.

We weren't outside long when Jean noticed the signs of tent moths invading the top of an old cherry tree that adorned the side of my house. The problem needed attention right away or, according to Jean, the tree would soon be destroyed.

Jean sounded the alarm, and Frank and I were on the case. It wasn't just the tree that needed protecting. Our honor was at stake. Our reputation. There was practically no construction or landscaping challenge Frank and I couldn't handle—and Jean knew that from the years Frank helped me restore my house, a simple Quaker structure built in the 1830s.

Chiseling through stone walls. Digging footings and constructing fencing. Hauling gravel and concrete and tree stumps. Jackhammering basement floors to install sump pumps. Replacing doors, siding and staircases. Underpinning foundations in the crawl space. Frank and I worked on many projects together. It was a way of putting everyday stresses behind us, and uncovering moments when, through hard physical work, mutual effort achieves a measure of perfection, even if it is reflected in something as simple as a re-routed water line or a new support to replace a rotted post.

Frank was a true artisan. Dexterous in hand, he was guided by a delicate sensibility. He may not have been Italian, but he had that fine Italian touch one associates with the best designers. Frank didn't learn carpentry and construction in a hair salon, of course. He learned it from Trig. Trig was legend. If you knew Frank, you knew Trig.

Trig was a cantankerous but lovable do-it-your-selfer and all-around mountain man who lived in a cabin in the Adirondacks. Pamela, a former girlfriend of Frank's, had a house outside of Saratoga. That's where Frank met Trig, and the two hit it off. Working alongside him, Frank mastered woodworking and construction. Trig would wake Frank at the break of dawn. In his gravelly voice, between puffs on a pipe packed with cedar-infused tobacco, Trig would shout, "Hey, what do you think this is, the city? We don't sleep late around here!" It didn't matter if Frank was feeling tired or under the weather. Trig didn't tolerate crybabies. One cold winter, Trig died of a heart attack hauling wood back to his cabin. He was in his seventies. Frank lost a dear friend, but it didn't end their dialogue. Not by a long shot. He spoke to the dearly departed Trig as if he were right next-door, ready to lend a hand. That sounds a bit crazy. I didn't quite understand it at the time. But I would later.

Before taking on a tough job at my house, Frank would say, "I wonder what Trig would do?" During the work, if it went well, Frank would be sure to say,

"Thanks, Trig." When the work was completed, Frank would burn some cedar incense as a show of gratitude. And in the morning, whenever Frank was hanging out at my place, he'd yell into my room, "What do you think this is, the city? We don't sleep late around here!" I never met Trig, but I certainly got to know him through Frank.

The tent moths Jean noticed didn't present much of a challenge. Under her watchful eye, Frank and I moved a ladder around the base of the tree. While Frank supported the ladder, I reached up from the top step with a fifteen-foot clipper to cut away any signs of the invaders. Then I sealed the bugs and branches in a heavy plastic bag. The tree was saved. The powerful duo that was Frank and me could cross another labor off our list.

With the sun about to make its first major appearance of the day, Jean and I strolled over to the swimming pool where we watched Frank perform back flips off the diving board, and sink twenty-foot pool hoops from the air. He was in the zone.

Sunday evening Frank went to sleep early and Jean and I stayed up talking outside. "Goodnight pal," he said. "See you tomorrow," and with that he headed up to the small guest room at the front of the house that had become his.

There was a quiet softness in the air as Jean and I continued talking outside.

"Do you know when I was going through chemo Frank trimmed my wig to make it look more natural?" Jean offered, rather suddenly. "He even added a few cowlicks so it would look more like my own."

"That's Frank," I said. "Always doing surprising things for people."

"I know," Jean agreed, laughing. "When I go anywhere with Frank, I leave an extra twenty minutes for all the good deeds he'll do for people on the way." Then Jean picked up Frank's Appalachian Trail book he brought to show his route, "I'm glad he's finally doing something for himself."

You would never expect it from a kid who grew up a few blocks from the Queensborough Bridge, but Frank's connection to the natural world was genuine. He could identify the song and flight of birds, and the species of flowers and trees. Every bug he met in my house, ladybugs, box-elder bugs, bees and spiders, was safely escorted outside. The introduction of the habitat-stealing starling to North America was the only thing that upset him more than callous commuters. And when the red-tail hawks were circling above my house—and there always seemed to be more when Frank was around—he would look up and shout, "Hey, Tommy!" That was the name he gave his soaring guides. It was easy to imagine Frank as a full-fledged mountain man hiking the Appalachian Trail, allowing nothing to disturb his meditation along the few remaining wild areas of the eastern seaboard.

Still, nothing Jean and I discussed even remotely pointed to the events that were about to unfold, or helped uncover why Frank had been so intent on bringing us together. But he had. When Frank chimed "goodnight" there was a sense of closure. Mission accomplished. While for Jean and me an unresolved chord hung in the air. It remained up to Frank to provide the answer we had been listening for all night.

It was getting late. Along with Frank's trail book, an empty bottle of wine and a few scattered items, Jean and I gathered the remains of the evening and headed inside. While she went to bed, I stayed up to unwind over a round of online chess.

A few moves into the game, I heard a noise coming from the laundry room. A metallic PING measured periodically against a long ROLLING sound. A dot with an extra-long dash. The dryer was emitting a strange signal. I opened it and found the source. It was Frank's marble. It had rolled loose from his pocket and was circling inside the dryer where he had tossed a load of wash before heading off to bed.

If you knew Frank, you knew his marble.

Among the few items Frank cared about, his marble had a place at the top. He called it a marble, but we were never quite sure. It could easily pass for a round quartz stone.

Frank discovered it in the dirt in the crawl space under my house. In order to gain headroom to insulate some outside walls and run new water and electric lines, Frank and I spent a few weekends removing dirt from the crawl space. Along the way we unearthed an old cistern. While its utility was long passed, it retained a venerable aspect because of its age and symmetry. In its very center, resting in the dirt more than a foot below the level from where we started excavating, Frank found the marble.

I turned the dryer back on and placed the marble in a cup on the table in the kitchen so Frank could get it in the morning, then returned to my game.

Monday morning came soon enough. Frank had managed to minimize his working hours, and Jean was in business for herself. Since they were in no rush to get back to New York, it was up to me to initiate the start of the day, get them to the station, and myself to work at the expected hour, plus whatever time my position tacitly allowed.

Before leaving the house, Frank would take a last look around. The pine tree he planted a few years before, which he nurtured from a sapling he got in the mail, was one of the spots he visited. He was always delighted at how quickly it grew since we moved it one weekend from his patio in Queens. He'd pull the weeds around it and give it some water if necessary.

Jean and Frank were waiting by the car when I stepped outside. Frank took a deep inhalation of fresh air as if to last him till the next visit. "Namaste," he said, clapping his hands together in gratitude, before we all got in the car. I drove them to the station for their return trip to NY, then on to work. But in the morning rush, I forgot to return the marble to Frank and he left without it.

Halfway through that work week, I came home to a brief message. It was Jean. "Michael, call me," she said, "It's about Frank." That whole day didn't sit well with me and I knew it couldn't be good news. The Wednesday morning following his visit Frank died of a heart attack during his morning swim at the Astoria pool. He was pronounced dead in the ambulance on the way to the hospital.

I sat in stunned silence as Jean talked about Frank's death. No other event has the power to so swiftly alter our sense of self and our connection with loved ones. Sadness, anger, shock, it all rose up with the sudden news of the loss of my friend, and the realization that everything is as temporary as the fizz in a San Pellegrino. Frank was a soulful person who connected with his destiny. He lived fifty-seven years. The weekend that had just passed was his "good bye." And he couldn't have said it better. That is what I came to accept soon after his death.

CHAPTER 2

...who gets excited by a mere penny?
— Annie Dillard

The following morning I called my office and told them I would not be coming in for a few days, that a close friend of mine had died.

I spent much of the remainder of that week making phone calls to Frank's friends at the request of his sister, Barbara. With every call, I experienced the stunned silence and grief at the news as if I was hearing it for the first time. His friends' sadness was my own. It is said we are all connected at the heart. Clearly that is so. After speaking further with Barbara, I decided to write a eulogy to honor Frank at his funeral service planned for Sunday afternoon, following the viewing. His burial was scheduled the next day.

I struggled with what to share about Frank. In a city restless for achievement, prestige was something Frank avoided. He had no attachment to property or things. He was content to take a seat in the wings, serving his clientele with nothing more than candidness, amusing conversation, and a good, precise trim.

Thursday, late afternoon, the day after Frank's death, the blackout of 2003 struck Manhattan. Millions of people were inconvenienced by this outage that enveloped the city in darkness, stopping trains and elevators and even traffic through the evening and into the next day. Most of Frank's friends lived in and around New York and couldn't be reached.

For a moment it occurred to me that Frank himself was behind it, that he finally got some revenge on a place he found less than hospitable. All those train rides and piled up resentments from living in tight spaces around careless people. Now he had the opportunity to exercise some redemptive energy. And with a far greater power authority on his side than Con Edison, he was in a position to pull it off.

That same afternoon a friend of mine, Amelia, who often hung around with us, stopped by my house to see how I was doing. Amelia and I sat outside by the pool where just days before Frank was relaxed and carefree. "If Frank's been around," I told her, "he hasn't given me a sign yet."

"Shhhhh," she whispered in the next instant. "Turn around."

There, sitting atop the fence that Frank and I spent so many months reconstructing, was an Eastern Bluebird. If Frank had a favorite bird, that was it. In all the years he visited, neither he nor I, nor Amelia, had ever seen one. I didn't know then, but it was just the beginning of an impressive and coordinated demonstration, one that defies space and time and leads to the inevitable conclusion that our souls never die, and that our friends and loved ones who have passed are there for us if we learn to listen.

It was now Sunday morning, August 16th, four days since Frank's death and the day of his service. I woke up with the sudden realization that I hadn't returned Frank's marble. As I mentioned, the marble had rolled loose in the dryer from where it telegraphed its PING-PING. I rushed downstairs hoping to find it. It was still there, in the cup where I placed it a week before.

I resolved then to return the marble to Frank. I felt glad that I had it because I knew what it meant to him. Had his sister or anyone else who didn't maintain close ties with Frank discovered it, its significance would have been lost.

I reduced the font size of the eulogy I wrote so it would fit on one page and folded it around the marble. Then I wrapped the package in plastic film and folded gift paper around that. I'm not very meticulous about such things and the result was not exactly Martha Stewart. However, while the package wasn't picture perfect, I sensed, just prior to wrapping Frank's marble, a perfect opportunity, which occurred so spontaneously that I didn't stop to think about it. Was there more beyond, *plus ultra*, this thing called life? I took the opportunity to find out. I hastily scribbled a note at the top of the eulogy: *"If you're ever around, toss this back."*

At the time, I never fully considered what it would mean if Frank did toss it back. Other than confirming that there isn't a hard stop after death, and that some aspect of our being endures. Neither did I question whether I was ready for a response. Nevertheless, I prepared the invitation and would deliver it myself. If anyone could provide answers, I knew it would be Frank.

David Bohm, a renowned physicist, posited a multidimensional universe enfolded upon itself. A hidden, infinite dimension where matter and consciousness share the same source. Information is present everywhere, as in a holographic plate, and reveals itself, a bit of matter at a time, as a tiny ripple on a vast ocean of energy. Later, I would think of Frank's marble, folded in a letter, folded in his pocket, and all of it, including Frank, folded into the ground from where, reaching its source, and directed by a greater consciousness, it would unfold again, and again, as needed, delivering the requested information.

Sunday morning was beautiful and sun drenched, exactly the kind of morning Frank and I would get an early start on a project when he was out for a visit. Now, I was preparing to see him, say a few words on his behalf and return the marble that I had every reason to believe would reside with him forever.

In the mid 19th century, Ludwig Büchner, a philosopher, physician, and avowed muckraker of spiritualists, wrote, "...any discussion of philosophic problems which cannot be brought into unison with the results obtained by science, is worthless and senseless." Today, Büchner might be astounded to learn that science and spirituality, while not blissfully united, are no longer poles apart. Indeed, what is often perceived as marginal has a sneaky way of gaining ground, like Van Goghs and Chia Pets. How far, for example, does the quantum world extend into the everyday world of things? There are no road signs along the way. But there are other signs. And those more spiritually inclined have been pointing them out for thousands of years. While some may say it's a stretch or even ignorant to attempt it, some rather surprising events can be brought in line with today's scientific insights. Should we care?

Some theories of how the world works seem far removed from our everyday lives to make a difference. If that's how you see it, stop and consider this: What if quantum events, which are supposed to reside at unimaginably minute levels, spilled over into your life at every moment? What if your present influenced the past? And objects that entered your life seemed intimately connected to other objects great distances away? What if vital information seemed to come at the last second, confirming intuitions about intuitions, and changing the outcome? What if the inevitable conclusion was that the universe was seeking a dialogue with you? Or rather, was in dialogue with you? Even playing with you? And your resources were its resources, your playthings, its playthings. And anything could serve as a means to exchange information. What then? Would you seek some answers? Make some adjustments? What kind?

At the time I was preparing for Frank's funeral service, I had no reason to entertain such thoughts. None whatsoever. Frank's marble was neatly folded in my suit pocket and ultimately bound for his. That was my goal. That, and pick up Amelia at her house in New Jersey, then drive to Manhattan where Gwen would join us.

In many ways Gwen's relationship with Frank parallels my own and Jean's. Gwen was a client who found herself drawn to Frank as a friend. It was a relationship they maintained for many years.

For Gwen and Jean, a thirty-minute haircut could turn into a three-hour discussion about the virtues of high colonics or the plight of Himalayan leopards. Paula, the owner of the salon, would listen, at times amused, at times in frustration, as a relatively expensive piece of New York real estate, i.e. her salon chair, was suddenly consumed by sweeping tales of imminent catastrophes, natural and otherwise. Western civilization was in its steepest decline, and as far as Frank was concerned there was no stopping it.

I would take a more optimistic view, and argue with Frank about such prophecies, how the world had heard them before and was still around. There was no dissuading him. Few of us are prepared to step into the darkness of our own being to determine why we may need to construct such a pessimistic outlook. Frank was too dear a friend for me to challenge him on that basis. But I knew all too well how trauma could color one's world.

As Amelia and I drove up Eighth Avenue to pick up Gwen, the skies of Manhattan began to darken. It was raining heavily when we reached Jane Street in Greenwich Village. We were early, so I stopped in a deli around the corner from Gwen's place to get some water, and waited for her under an awning.

Gwen adored Frank and felt torn apart by the news of his death. She remembers how, just hearing his name the evening I called, she knew he was gone. And I remember thinking she would. Frank and Gwen went out to dinner the week before. He showed up at Gwen's house with a number of gifts, including a book of poetry.

Frank had been through AA and was approaching his twentieth anniversary of sobriety. One night on the Long Island Expressway, Frank was driving drunk and flipped his car over at high speed. He had just put twenty coats of lacquer on his car. It was immaculate. That's when Frank was working as a body and fender man. Frank woke up in a ditch, covered in dirt. Amazingly, he was okay. But his car was totaled. "I raised myself up from the mud," he said. He got into AA and never took another drink. He let his driver's license expire and didn't get another. As he put it, "From then on I let God steer my life."

With the recent passing of his mother, Frank was having a rough time making the transition from caregiver to caring more for himself. He was freer than he had ever been, but, according to Gwen, he was frightened and awed by the prospect.

Frank struggled with all this. But there was a bright spot. He was falling in love with Luz, a nurse's assistant who had helped look after his mother. Luz was eliciting in Frank genuine feelings of love after so many years of living without it. Only she was not quite ready to respond to Frank in the way he would have wished.

"I feel like my heart is breaking," Frank told Gwen, his words falling on her heart with a tenderness she had never heard. The death of his mother, the pressure he felt to sell the house and begin his journey, sadness at Luz's hesitation to commit to a deeper relationship—it was all weighing on him.

Gwen looked at her dinner with Frank through the same lens as I looked at the weekend that followed. Ostensibly, Frank was preparing for a long hike. Beneath it all he was letting go, parting with the few meaningful possessions he had, preparing his goodbye. While Gwen was almost twenty years younger than Frank, their age difference was never important to her. "But that night," she said, "he looked older, as if time was catching up."

A few nights after their dinner, Frank called Gwen to tell her he was bringing Jean to my house. "They *have* to meet," he said. "It's very important." But he didn't say why. And he added, "Don't worry about my umbrella. I'll get it the next time I see you." It was raining hard when Gwen walked around the corner. She was under Frank's umbrella. "I've never felt more protected," she said.

We arrived at the funeral home in Queens a little early. I took the opportunity to place the small packet with Frank's marble inside his suit jacket. It was the same suit Frank had purchased for his mother's funeral three months before. I touched his shoulder, closed my eyes and thought about all the times he was there for me. I was looking at my friend in the last place you'd ever want to see one. And realized how absurd that would sound if I actually spoke that thought, like something Yogi Berra might say when death has made itself tragically apparent.

There was forty minutes before the start of the service. Amelia, Gwen, and I went outside and walked around the corner where we found a tavern. We sat around the bar and sipped some wine delivered in respectful silence. Compared to the artificial décor of the funeral home, the bar felt like a more hallowed place. In short order we made our way back to the mortuary where a crowd was gathering. A priest made a hurried entrance and took his place at the front of the room. It was hard to believe anyone "in the business" could act as inured to the sadness that accompanies such a loss as the pastor who was standing before us.

"Frank deserves something more than the Lord's Prayer recited like it was a 50-yard dash," Jean whispered to me. Either Frank's sister hadn't given the priest much to go on, or he hadn't bothered to ask. Either way, it seemed like the service was designed in the interest of expediency rather than honoring Frank's life. That reality would confront us again on the next day during the drive to the cemetery.

I was glad Jean, Gwen, and I had prepared something in Frank's memory. Given the speed of the benediction, it was only a matter of minutes when it became our turn to reclaim a legacy of friendship and caring that had been so swiftly disregarded by the hollow words that flew by.

Jean spoke first. This was the Frank we knew. The guy who went out of his way to be kind. A lover of nature who created a wild life sanctuary in his back yard, grew a vegetable garden and fed chickadees from his hand. Jean spoke lovingly of those moments when Frank was there for her, supporting and encouraging her through the most trying period of her life, never once making her feel awkward or uncomfortable during her long months of chemotherapy.

Gwen spoke next. Meeting Frank for the first time was for her an instant recognition of a deeper connection. Like Jean, she'd felt cared for and supported in his presence. When Gwen began writing poetry and attending readings, Frank was her biggest fan.

It was my turn. I was determined to deliver a message that was clear and faithful to Frank's spirit. As I read my statement, I felt Frank was with me, sharing the weight of that moment, helping me yet again in his completely unselfish manner carry a sadness that stretched across space and time into another dimension from where now, and perhaps always, he would dwell.

There was utter quiet after we spoke. The person Jean, Gwen, and I talked about was the man people knew Frank to be. After the service, we had dinner at one of Frank's favorite restaurants near his house. Italian, of course. I chose that moment to tell Jean, Gwen, and Amelia about Frank's marble, how I had returned it to him a few hours earlier. Everyone knew its significance and was glad Frank had it back. None of us gave it much thought beyond that.

Frank's burial was scheduled at Calverton National Cemetery the next morning. Calverton is a veteran's cemetery on Long Island about an hour and a half from New York City. Frank had been a helmsman in the Navy Reserves and was proud of his service. It was a fitting place for him to rest. Gwen, Amelia, and I stayed overnight at a hotel near La Guardia airport so we could attend the burial service. Jean needed to get home for a meeting the next day and couldn't join us.

I didn't sleep well that night. The next morning I met Gwen and Amelia in the hotel lobby where there was a small breakfast buffet of miniature muffins and Danish that only needed another second or two of exposure to fully qualify as stale.

Befitting the tenor of the morning, Amelia and I were having an argument. In her early morning wandering she came across three pennies. "Heads up," she said. She was convinced this was an acknowledgment from Frank. I questioned such a quotidian display and the conclusion she drew. "Surely," I said to Amelia, "if Frank were around, he would find a more impressive way to announce his presence than tossing a few pennies on the ground."

"That's your opinion," Amelia shot back.

"What about the bluebird we saw at my house," I said, breaking off a piece of stale muffin. "That was a far more convincing demonstration. Don't you think? Besides," I added, "there are pennies everywhere. People get rid of them because they're not worth...a penny. They're a nuisance. If you are looking for pennies the odds are you're going to find one."

"Not so," argued Amelia, shaking her head, offering no further support for her position than her own belief that the most ubiquitous of coins, discovered in the most populated of places, could demonstrate the presence of a departed soul.

"Hallelujah!" I conceded. "Comfort in a penny. If it makes you happy, so be it."

Reasoning with Amelia could be daunting. If anyone belonged in a mid-19th century séance room with thick velvet curtains and the smell of candle wax, it was she. Don't attempt to argue rationally with anyone so dominated by the feeling function, more than one Jungian analyst has warned. But with respect to Amelia, I fell for that trap every time. The exchange rate she put forth, a penny for your soul, or, at least, the presence of one, didn't sit well with me. And I took issue with it, because the soul she was referring to was Frank's.

Curiously, Frank and Amelia were born on the same day, November 14. They had much in common. Both were outdoors people and expert birders who also enjoyed gardening. Amelia's dad, however, was really Italian. But the truth is Frank never warmed up to her, to put it mildly. While he always found something to be cheerful about, Amelia is one of those people who complains regularly, who laments the lack of joy in her life. This she has brought to a high art. She can sense the damage in someone's soul and infiltrate their shadow. Once breached, she will assume some of the burden, such that the recipient feels a debt of gratitude without knowing why. I have experienced this trick myself. As a result, Amelia frequently becomes the person you love to hate. Of course, she doesn't deserve that. It is not a formula for lasting friendship, but knowing someone like Amelia allows you to discover what you may need to fix in yourself. Frank would have none of that. For him, being around Amelia was as comfortable as wearing a hairshirt. The fact that she was along for the second day of this mournful journey made me sensitive to what would have been his considerations. So now you can appreciate my discomfort when I listened to how

Frank was supposedly dropping pennies from heaven and Amelia was scooping them up. I found it hard to believe, unless in death Frank had a moment of conversion, and his animosity for her lifted.

We picked up our bags and headed for the hotel parking lot. I remember scanning the pavement for lost coins. Had I found one, I would have raised it to the heavens and shouted, "Look, a penny! Frank is alive and well on the other side!" We got in the car and headed up Grand Central Parkway to the funeral home and were soon stuck in traffic. I opened the door.

"What are you doing?" Amelia asked.

"Looking for pennies!" I said.

We all laughed. Now, at least, the pennies gained a little more value in providing some comic relief.

We reached the funeral home before Frank's sister and a few other members of her family arrived. Gwen and Amelia went inside while I waited out front. It wasn't long before Luz walked up, the nurse's assistant with whom Frank had fallen in love.

I met Luz at the funeral of Frank's mother. And here we were just a few months later at his. Luz was from Columbia and Frank had been helping her with her English. She was quite lovely. I could see why Frank was taken with her. They had spent a summer's day at the beach just a couple of weeks before. She spoke about that day, how Frank had expressed "the most beautiful words to me any man has ever said."

Luz was one of the first people to hear the news. She woke up that Wednesday morning with the feeling she needed to call him. She got anxious when there was no answer on his cell phone. Then she got a call

back from the same number. But it wasn't Frank. It
was a police detective. He was investigating Frank's
death. It was his job to rule out anything other than
natural causes. He wanted to know if Luz was a family
member. "Who is this?" she said. "What happened to
Frankie?"

"I can't tell you," the detective said. He needed the
name of a family member. Luz gave him Frank's sister's number and then called the hospital near Frank's
house. "He was here," they told her, "in the emergency
room."

"Are you family?" they asked. Luz didn't want to
lie. "That's all we can tell you."

Frank's sister called Luz and confirmed the worst.
Luz had maintained a warm and caring relationship
with Frank's mother. Now her son was gone, too, just
when Luz was starting to realize what a special soul he
was. Luz and I walked into the funeral home together.

It was Monday and there were fewer mourners
around than the previous day. When his sister Barbara
arrived, she extended an invitation to ride with her in
the limo to Calverton. It was a nice offer. But I didn't
say yes immediately. It needed some consideration.

I knew Frank had a number of differences with his
sister over the years. It revolved around Frank assuming
the burden of caregiving for his mother, and feeling his
sister did nothing to help. It's odd sharing the death of
your friend with someone you know he didn't like very
much. Barbara would make two, when you include
Amelia. But at least Amelia liked Frank. I had come to
see a friend laid to rest, and to remember. Barbara was
there to bury her guilt, and to forget. And the sooner,

the better. That was increasingly apparent.

Still, I remained undecided. Continue the journey with Gwen and Amelia, or accept Barbara's offer for all of us to ride with her? I felt remorse for Barbara, and didn't want to disappoint her. On the other hand, this would be my last ride with Frank. I was more inclined to spend it sharing memories of Frank with friends who would miss him, rather than feeling trapped in a limo behind smoky glass, pretending everything had been okay with his sister. Then the thought occurred to me, let Frank decide.

I walked back into the room and asked Amelia if I could borrow her pennies. If her position wasn't validated, at least now her pennies were getting some attention. I returned to the waiting area where Gwen and I put the question to Frank.

"Okay, Frank," I said looking at Gwen. "Heads we drive in my car. Tails we ride in the limo with your sister. You decide."

It didn't occur to us at that moment how absurd it looked, flipping pennies in a funeral home waiting for the deceased to render an opinion about which car we should take to his funeral. Frank, however, would have been delighted in our continuation of the penny motif. It was just the kind of running gag that would characterize our friendship, becoming part of our history. Of course, in retrospect, it was right on point, providing space for the universe to inch this story along. A story which, as yet, showed no signs of becoming anything more than the gathering of friends and family, rocked by anguish and regret at the loss of a loved one, and the irrepressible fact that we are each in our own way marching to the same sad finale. And that is an old story indeed.

We tossed three pennies. The first came up heads. The second, tails. We tossed the third penny for definitive word. Heads again. Two bits "yes." One bit, "no."

Weeks later, I would apologize to Amelia for my smug attitude about her penny finds. After all, I realized, there was no reason the same operative laws that I felt were supporting my convictions couldn't support hers. "Information is information," wrote Werner R. Loewenstein, an expert on biophysics, "whether it is carried by atomic nuclei, molecules, or the balls of an abacus." To Loewenstein's list I would add Amelia's pennies...and another small spherical object, which was about to make its presence known.

There were more tearful moments before Frank's casket was closed. With Luz in the room, it was hard not to reflect on the happiness that may have awaited them were Frank still alive. But another quick reading of the Lord's Prayer brought a solemn end to that thought. The brief service was over. Our small contingent filed out and gathered in the waiting area. From there I noticed the funeral director preparing to close Frank's casket. Something called me back.

"My friend was always interested in mechanical things," I said, with no better explanation for returning to the room.

"Oh really," the funeral director responded, without looking up.

"Yes, he was fascinated." I said.

Frank was in many ways an engineer at heart. He would record Nova and Discovery documentaries of bridges and buildings going up and all sorts of technical marvels.

I quickly realized, however, what led me back. I had returned to witness the staging of what, if Frank could pull it off, would be a miracle. This was the do-or-die moment when the assistant locks the magician in the box encircled by thick chains. Of course, it was too late for Frank to get out alive. But what about the marble I placed in his pocket? Could that escape? And why was I entertaining such preposterous ideas anyway? Still, I was enthralled.

My father had been an accomplished amateur magician. He was a big hit in the army during WWII, entertaining wounded soldiers on a hospital ship that sailed between England and the U.S. They dubbed him, "The Great Eldini." Besides his greatest and most audacious act, concealing sadism and pedophilia under the cloak of Mister Nice Guy, he could perform mind-reading tricks and complex memory feats, like remembering long number chains. As the funeral director prepared to close Frank's casket, performing his routine with the assurance of someone who had done it a thousand times, I was feeling that sense of childish wonder, as one might have before Harry Houdini was sealed inside a packing crate and dumped into the East River.

"How does that close?" I asked the director.

I watched him slide the long steel bolts through a barrel that dovetailed with the top and sides of the casket, then engage the locking mechanism. If you believed the manufacturer's claim, it would keep air and moisture out forever. Or at least substantially

longer than any living person might be around to
check. I was satisfied that the marble I placed inside
Frank's suit pocket would remain just where it was,
forever.

Now, instead of riding with Barbara inside the
limo, Gwen, Amelia, and I followed in my car, just as
our penny tosses decreed. With the hearse leading our
procession, we drove by Frank's house on 31st Street
in Astoria. The big ceramic donkey from Mexico that
Frank used as a planter was still in front, chained to
the fence. Frank had taken that protective measure
after some kid tried to steal it. We headed south to the
entrance of the Grand Central Parkway and the drive
to Calverton.

Padmasambhava was the Indian sage who brought
Buddhism to Tibet over a thousand years ago. Legend
has it that he vanquished the demons that stood in the
way of enlightenment. Trig-unadhara, a minister in the
court of King Indrabodhi, discovered Padmasambhava as a small child in the center of a white lotus on an
island in a jeweled lake.

I used to joke with Frank, whose last name was
Bava, which in Sanskrit means "new soul" or "becoming," about changing his name to Bava-sambhava as a
way to inspire him to vanquish his own demons. That
Padmasambhava was discovered by a fellow named
"Trig," the name of Frank's cedar-smoking friend in
Saratoga, added amusement, if not weight, to the name
change. Although Frank never officially changed his
name to Bava-sambhava, he loved it. One day we were
in a Home Depot and I'd lost him somewhere in the
store. I went to the front and asked if they could page

my friend. "Sure," the teenager at the checkout said, "what's his name?"

"Bava-sambhava." I said.

"Huh?" came the reply. I said the name again and we practiced it a few times. He was ready for the big announcement.

Amidst the hubbub of a weekend crowd with shopping carts laden with paint and wood and glue and all the materials we patch together to keep our homes safe and comfortable, Home Depot suddenly echoed with the hallowed name of an Indian sage, or at least a close facsimile.

"Would Ba-vah-sum-bah-vah please come to the front?"

I saw Frank bounding down the aisle, smiling all the way.

The chant of bava-sambhava was now washing over us in my car as I turned up the volume. It was a song by Deep Forest, called "Bohemian Ballet," in a CD titled *Boheme* that Frank and I frequently listened to. The chorus sounded exactly like "Bava-sambhava." And I blasted that section—Bava-Bavasambhavaaa!, Bava-Bavasambhavaaa!—trying as best I could to expel my sadness as we approached the entrance to the Long Island Expressway.

As the chorus faded, our discussion drifted to Frank's attraction to Luz. While Frank had been pursuing her, Gwen and I had been cast in the role of advisors. Now we had an opportunity to compare notes. It was amusing to discover how different Gwen's advice was from mine.

I was in the go-for-it camp. "Don't hold back."

"This is great news." "What are you waiting for?"

"Don't listen to Michael," Gwen cautioned Frank. "What does he know about relationships?" There was no disputing that. Gwen advised Frank against rushing into anything, urging him to give Luz and himself more time to see what developed between them.

But now we were the ones who seemed to be rushing, speeding, rather. My eye caught the dashboard. We were traveling close to 90 mph!

"Why is the limo driving so fast?" I shouted.

We were heading east in the left lane, trailing behind the limo that was following the hearse. Suddenly, my car lost power.

I cannot exaggerate the danger. As my car slowed, other cars were speeding past. With no power to accelerate, and just a guardrail on my left, I had to wait for a hole in traffic to drift over to the shoulder on my right, four lanes away. With my emergency lights flashing, I managed to get into the next lane. I was slowing rapidly, however, and with every second of delay the risk of someone slamming into us became more imminent.

I barely made it to the next lane, but with two more to go, there was no chance of making it safely to the service lane. We were at a complete standstill in the middle of the Expressway. I was sure a car was going to slam into us and prepared for the impact. I flashed on a mountain of twisted metal across the highway, our flesh embedded in the debris.

The car behind me sounded its horn and screeched to a halt, just short of a crash. But we weren't out of danger. Not yet. We were still stuck in the middle of the road with cars speeding by, left and right. Then, from out of nowhere, a car casually pulled up on the passenger side, stopped, and calmly rolled down the window, as if it were a lovely spring morning.

In the most peaceful, ethereal voice I ever heard, the driver of the car asked, "How can we help you?" There was a passenger beside him, his gaze focused on a distant horizon, not the ground on which we were so precariously placed.

The driver's words seemed to float in the air. I was so taken with his unheralded presence, and the sweetness of his voice, that I didn't know how to respond. In stark contrast to the stress we were feeling in the car, he exuded calm. I could see that Gwen and Amelia were having trouble taking it all in, too. It didn't seem possible, this sudden rescue. Cars were speeding past in the same lane as theirs a moment before, yet they pulled alongside my car without any fear of anyone slamming into them. It was a feat of extraordinary timing. I looked up at the driver, who was patiently waiting for a response.

"Can you give us a push?"

"Push?" he said, in the same distinctive voice in which he offered help. "Sure, we can push," he said, trying not to smile, glancing at his silent friend, as if he had heard it all before.

My car, an Audi wagon, is one of the heavier cars on the road. We were stuck on an incline, and I wondered how they were ever going to push the car up the slope without additional help. I turned to Gwen in the backseat and asked her to take the wheel so I could get out and join them. But I didn't have to. Before I could get out of my car, they were already out of theirs, with

no sign of trepidation as they faced a rush of oncoming
cars speeding past. In the next instant, we were moving
effortlessly up the incline to a painted divider on our
right, safely out of traffic.

Clearly they had some muscle behind them. But
the strength required to push the car, given its weight
and how it was situated, would seem to present a bigger
challenge than anything they could handle. Yet they
accomplished the task with ease, and as soon as they
were done, sped away. The scene moved from push to
departure, instantaneously. As much as I wanted to say
thanks, there wasn't space for it.

I was a music major in college. I knew an elision
when I heard one, when distinct sections overlap. But
I'd never seen one, except in the movies, or manufac-
tured in an editing room, or maybe, in a dream. Our
two friends were not just fast, they were defying time,
as if they had the ability to operate from outside it.
Remarkable strength, astounding facility, and gone
before you know it. That is the cliché when it comes to
angels, isn't it? And in their repertoire of miracles, I had
asked for the most pedestrian of all, a push. No wonder
they were amused.

And the party wasn't over yet. Gwen and I noticed
a woman in black, dressed in a gossamer-like costume,
a flowing sort of Victorian piece, standing on the side of
the road. Our view of her was fleeting, like the glimpse
of a hummingbird darting before a feeder. But it was
long enough to catch her directing traffic and waving
good-bye to our friends, whom she acknowledged as
one might a co-worker, as if saying, "Good job, fellas. See you at the next one." Gwen and I assumed the

apparition was Amelia, who was also dressed in a kind of flowing black ensemble. But it wasn't. Later, when I told Amelia how glad I was that she was able to thank the men, she looked puzzled.

"Thank *who?*" she asked.

Amelia had never stood in the road, waving good-bye to anyone. The woman in black was not Amelia. As soon as the men stopped beside us, she jumped out of the car and ran up the service road to speak with the driver of the limo, who had pulled off when he saw we were in trouble.

The limo driver's name was Tommy. We didn't realize that either, until later, when we noticed his name above the cell phone number he scribbled on a piece of paper and handed to us.

"Don't worry," Tommy said, "I was looking out for you." I'm not sure how driving 90 mph was looking out for us. Nevertheless, when I recalled his name, I thought of the soaring hawks that flew over my house when Frank was around, all of whom he called, "Tommy."

Gwen and I were now in the car resting on the painted divider. I tried starting the car again and suddenly it came to life. I looked at Gwen and we shrugged it off. There are just so many wonders you can accept in a morning. We drove up the service road where the limo was waiting. Since my car was running again, and we were only twenty minutes from the cemetery, we continued on, traveling slowly in the right lane just in case something happened.

We arrived at the cemetery fifteen minutes later without further incident. Wooded, green, stretching over a thousand acres far from the hustle-bustle of Queens, Calverton looked like an ideal resting place for Frank.

Final services were held in an outdoor pavilion. We parked on a quiet roadway and got out to stretch. It was a short walk to the pavilion, where two Navy Honor Guards in their summer whites were standing at attention on either side of Frank's casket, draped in an American flag.

With taps in the background, the Honor Guards performed the ceremony with grace and precision, pausing twelve times with another flag stretched between them to make each triangular fold. Then one of the Honor Guards kneeled before Frank's sister. Head bowed, with great dignity, he spoke a few words and presented the flag to Barbara as tears rolled down her face.

I was moved by this disciplined show. Yet I was also preoccupied by something else; something extraordinary. The Honor Guards were the same men who stopped to help Amelia, Gwen, and me. And when the lead Honor Guard, who reminded us of the driver, spoke in the same fluid and reassuring voice, we all looked at each other, our eyes wide with astonishment. They looked at us, too. Then, as before, quickly stepped away and vanished from the scene. Were they angels in disguise? Or simply two honor guards on the way to the same funeral? I tried to find the answer. A few days later I called the cemetery to see if I could learn their names. They said such duty was on a volunteer basis, and they had no record of who the men might be. So I didn't pursue it—largely because I would soon find myself consumed by other inexplicable events.

Still, today, I can't recall the sound of the driver's voice without tears in my eyes. There was something utterly peaceful in his bearing, and in his partner's. I sensed an infinite strength at their disposal. And something more, an effort not to upset the fabric of our illusion. The one that leaves open to question whether such beings truly exist. A *deus ex machina* was delivered center stage. Although they did their best, none of us were fooled by the charade. God sent some fine angels. They just weren't good actors. They dropped their masks. Or maybe, they were supposed to.

With the military observance completed, I stood with Gwen and Amelia to read a Buddhist prayer for Frank since he respected the Buddha's teachings. We prayed that he be reborn in a Pure Land of Joy, that he reach the highest ground of radiance, obtaining the prophecy of enlightenment for all sentient beings. If Frank was truly on the bodhisattva path, he would have made the most selfless vow imaginable. He would return in his next life to help others.

On the ride back to New York, I drove slowly and cautiously because of my concern about the car. A short distance from the Triborough Bridge, the one that connected Frank's neighborhood with Manhattan, I gave Jean a call to tell her about the funeral service. But it was Jean's news that grabbed the front page. When she got home Sunday evening there was an object waiting at her entrance: A clear marble, exactly like Frank's. Frank wasted no time "tossing it back." Jean was shocked, but had no doubt about who delivered it to her doorstep.

While everything that happened earlier—avoiding a serious accident, the good Samaritans who doubled as Frank's honor guards—seemed incredible, it didn't compare to the news Jean shared. A marble. Waiting by the entrance to her home in Brooklyn. Frank had pulled off a miracle.

CHAPTER 3

...chance is but the pseudonym of God
— M.G. Gupta

I was awestruck at Jean's news. And I've been that way ever since. It was a revelation that engendered an immediate change in my being.

I had asked of Frank a miracle, or at the least I opened the door for one. And though my request for him to "toss the marble back" had been hastily prepared, with no expectations, I received a quick and affirmative answer. That made it all the more astounding. Frank had indeed tossed the marble back. And although it landed on Jean's doorstep, given the distance it had to travel, it seemed close enough to me for the universe to register a "yes," confirming he was around.

It is not easy to speak of such an all-encompass-
ing shift, when one's awareness begins to orient around
a new dynamic, as if the polarity of the earth had
changed. With the news of Jean's find, I felt the power
of an enormous presence. I was trembling, like a child
pulled from a frozen lake. But this time the monster
in the room was not my father. It was something else.
And it was I who would need to adjust to it, not the
other way around. Now the urgency around Jean's
visit with Frank and the myriad events that led to her
discovery all made sense. In tossing the marble back,
Frank had struck the defining chord Jean and I were
listening for the evening the three of us spent together,
bringing coherence to everything before.

But what was that presence, the "monster" in the
room? I wasn't sure. One's Greater Self? A mere projection? A natural force to be reckoned with? A thunder-
ous calling? To what? And what, I wondered, becomes
of the receiver who, in disbelief or arrogance, ignores it?

When Gottfried Wilhelm Leibniz worked out the
binary system in the 17th century, he believed he had
found the secret to creation. The number "one," he pro-
posed, represented unity and stood for God. The zero
represented the void. "With one," he said, "everything
can be drawn from nothing." It was Leibniz who first
conceived the idea of a digital computer. What was at
the heart of his machine? Marbles. Leibniz used marbles to represent his binary numbers. They fed small
gates that were opened and closed, depending on the
number. Over 300 years ago the great Leibniz was
playing with marbles and mulling over the existence
of God. Now Frank, or Something, was serving up

a marble out of the ether. And like the Great Marble Calculating Machine envisioned by Leibniz, the variables seemed to fall into position, offering an astounding yet unmistakable result. And though I was hardly a pinball wiz, let alone a math one, I'd felt as lit up as the scoreboard in an arcade game when someone hits the jackpot.

Let it not be said, however, that there wasn't room for doubt. There always is. And I jumped in. Not as a cynic, but with the insistence of a rational being who seeks some plausible explanations. The Büchner in me needed a reason *not* to believe.

I called Jean the next day. I wanted to understand the material circumstances that contributed to her discovery of the marble. If there was a way of formulating a rational explanation, I wanted to know. While there was no altering the deep transitional experience I felt, I was willing to challenge that truth for the facts.

Jean lived in the garden apartment of a brownstone in Brooklyn Heights. Her entrance was under the stairs to the first floor of the building. There wasn't enough clearance under the stairs to have a screen door that opened out, so she used a fabric screen that attached to the top of the doorframe.

When Jean investigated the next day, at my request, she found the hem of the screen was weighted with, of all things, marbles as ballast. Jean noticed a tiny hole in the hem of the screen. Conceivably, that tiny hole could have allowed a marble to slip out and land on her cast iron filigree doormat.

Here was the million-dollar question: How did the marble emerge? From a tear in the fabric of Jean's screen? Or, from a tear in the fabric of our world? With the former explanation, the story would end right there. The marble simply leaked out onto her doormat, like a drop of water from a broken faucet. That was surely enough evidence to doubt the supernal quality of Jean's discovery. And thank God, the one I almost fully accepted. Life is demanding enough without having to acknowledge celestial forces lurking behind every event, and living like 14th century Christian monks, under a cumbrous "Cloud of Unknowing," or like Hassids or Hare Krishnas, in a constant state of propitiative awe.

I'm exaggerating a bit. I didn't foresee becoming a zealot of any persuasion. But just in case, with Jean's explanation I was off the hook. All this mishegoss about a marble. Now I could lose myself in the everyday, without questioning what I was missing, or what was beyond. I could continue my life and my little commute to my comfortable spot in corporate America without any regrets. I could get this marble off my back.

How did Jean feel about my questions? Irritated at the slightest doubt. Jean was a seasoned financial editor who professed to make a religion out of due diligence, at least where money was concerned. She bristled at the idea that the marble waiting on her doorstep was not 100% bonafide miraculous.

"The marble," she insisted, "was from Frank." Then she presented her case.

"First," she said, "it's different from the other marbles in the hem of the fabric screen. It's greenish, with an interior brush of dark green. All the marbles in the screen have no color or character whatsoever."

"Second, it was the way I found it. I felt something strange, right under my foot, as if it were alive. And then it was the way I saw it, shining in the light. I never doubted it came from Frank."

"Third, the chickadees." This took me by surprise. "Yes, the chickadees," she added with conviction.

"In fall and winter, they're plentiful," Jean continued. "But I heard only one in fall and one in spring. I wondered where they'd gone. I use to joke about these cheerful birds with Frank, even just recently at your place. The day after his death I heard one calling when I was thinking about what I was going to say at his service. It was the first time I'd heard a chickadee in months."

"And finally," Jean said, and with this I couldn't argue, "the fact that Frank pushed so hard to arrange the weekend we spent together." That alone was proof enough for Jean.

Okay, if you like tall tales, here was a good one: My friend dies. I return his prized marble to him just before his funeral and tuck it in his suit pocket with a note to toss it back if he's ever around. Then, a marble turns up that same evening at the entrance to a mutual friend's house, who, in fifteen years I had never met, but my friend was intent on bringing us together the weekend before he dies. The only evidence a logical person needs in order to shout "Hey, that's coincidence!" is a hem full of marbles at the base of a fabric screen with a tiny hole from which one could escape at just the right moment, to be falsely identified as a miraculous marble tossed from another space-time coordinate outside our own.

A short time later, I shared the story with a few coworkers. They were astonished. But what was even more astonishing was that, just three days later, what may have in the 19th century passed for an amusing parlor story, the kind Ludwig Büchner would dismiss with delight, began to grow into something more significant. Something that would effect further changes, not only in my life, but in the lives of those with whom I shared the story. Because many of these people would themselves come into possession of a marble or a round stone under extraordinary circumstances.

It was evident that this was a tale with many codas, like an ellipsis, each dot pulsating with life and energy. I was sensing the rhythm of a wave rolling on new shore where time itself, and everything in it, was becoming sacred. Leibniz's one was becoming many. Bits were turning into bytes. Sequences were being established. Redundancy was being introduced to overcome error. The universe wasn't just serving up a marble. It was starting a conversation.

A week after Jean returned home to find a marble, Frank's friend Gwen sent this email after she discovered one herself on a trip to Minnesota.

From: Gwen
Date: Sun, 24 Aug 2003 14:00:06 EDT
Subject: Bava beat me to Minneapolis

Hello all —
    I've just returned from my business trip and though bleary eyed and sleep deprived I

had to relay this ASAP.

Wednesday night in Minneapolis, I took two of my account managers to dinner, Janice and Deidre. Janice has become a close friend—both of them I trust. They knew I attended Bava's funeral on Monday and asked about it. I told them about the angels...then the story of the marble...how Bava found it at Michael's house and kept it always. How Michael heard it bouncing around in the dryer. Then, how Michael returned it to Bava, asking him to "toss it back if he was ever around." And, finally, how Jean found a similar one on her doorstep returning from the funeral home that Sunday night.

At one point during the story, Deidre, my account manager, yelled, "Oh God, I'm getting chills!" Her face went flush.

After I finished, Deidre said, "I got chills because Sunday evening when I was doing the laundry, I kept hearing a PING-PING-PING. When I took the clothes out, I found a clearish-blue marble with a green swirl, almost like a leaf." She had no idea where the marble had come from. She put it under the Tide cap and left it in her basement. Deidre gave me the marble—it's beautiful!

Even before my story, she'd been stunned as to how it appeared in her laundry. Late that night, after our dinner, she was telling Don, her boyfriend, about the marble and clarification came. Don had been doing yard work Sunday afternoon, digging, and found the marble in the dirt. He thought it odd and placed it in his pocket. Later, he threw his clothes in the wash—forgetting about the marble.

Deidre and Don believe the marble is from Frank. When the marble was handed to me, part of me couldn't take it in. But the more I look at the marble and hold it, I know it is from Frank. I've kept it with me since Thursday when I received it.

The fact that both marbles came on Sunday night and both have a green swirl is, well, beyond words. I know Frank's having a good laugh.

Let me know your thoughts. I'm looking forward to putting our marbles together.

Much love,

Gwen

Whatever doubts I had about the miraculous quality of Jean's marble were obliterated with Gwen's news. I know probability is a statistical tool to compensate for uncertainty, but if there is no doubt, who needs the tool? Nevertheless, this was new territory for me: A place where coincidence abandons any obligation to probability and becomes the partner of another reality, one that only the heart can fathom. Skeptics and quants (short for quantitative analysts) can attribute such claims to "magical thinking," to the "power of suggestion" or to the "statistics of large numbers." But who cares? Let them adjust their tables and interpret them however they choose.

And yet, still, I could hardly believe it myself. I felt as though I was losing my footing. I was feeling overwhelmed, as if I wasn't quite up to the game. I had barely survived my earthly father. And now I felt a greater authority recruiting me for something I wasn't quite sure. A "heavenly Father"? Doesn't He know I abhor anything that smacks of paternalism? Or was Frank the sole agent? These were impossible questions. You might as well ask a stone. So I did.

CHAPTER 4

The clear bead at the center changes everything
— Rumi

Were there one credible explanation beyond that of chance or coincidence to explain the emergence of Jean and Gwen's marbles, I would have embraced it heart and soul. Why? Because their appearance had become as much an irritant as consolatory.

Perhaps the marbles constituted clear evidence that the soul lives on. If Frank could operate on soul power, so conceivably could anyone. I suppose there is some comfort in that: the notion that it is not altogether over when we think it's supposed to be over, that death is not finality, that some part of our make-up is conserved. On the other hand, the rational side of my being sought some plausible explanation. To that end it seemed appropriate to examine what science could tell us, however makeshift it might be.

I could feel different sides of my being, the skeptic that didn't want to believe, and the believer who needed some rational basis to believe, taking up skirmish lines and marshaling different arguments. Yet each was not quite satisfied with its own point of view, while at the same time rejecting the other's. I was still looking at things from both sides of the coin, so to speak. And any peaceful resolution through some sort of meta-synthesis seemed far off.

Then too, there was another interior conflict brewing, based on the realization that, like my mother, I was evincing a kind of hypocrisy. Or denial. That I was not facing a truth. This, of course, was not pleasant to admit.

Let me explain. While both my parents professed to be socially conscious and culturally literate, I saw through their facade, and by extension their world, their friends, the books they read, and the art they hung on the walls. For what is the height of hypocrisy if not showcasing one's liberal values while vilely demoralizing one's child?

Of course, the deliberate cloaking of my father's dark deeds was more than hypocritical, it was pathological and hardly compares to quietly accepting some startling revelations of how, through the action of a few stray marbles, the world may really work. But, I argued, how is the mute acceptance of any powerful truth, even an evil one, much different, if that truth can answer, unequivocally, questions that have plagued us a long time? It seemed cowardly not to speak up about what was happening. I could see in the conflict between my wanting to believe and not quite allowing myself to believe, in God, or some higher purpose, the crux of my rationalization, and the mechanism for denial. My ambivalence was getting rather exhausting, and, I realized, only definitive action could resolve it.

My workplace, as it happened, was down the road from the modest two-story house on Mercer Street in Princeton where Albert Einstein once lived, and closer still to the Institute for Advanced Study where he consorted with other illustrious minds, like Kurt Gödel and Claude Shannon. Insofar as the world of science is concerned, it was one of Shannon's ideas that for me pointed to a promising area of inquiry.

Claude Shannon brought the world information theory. His work in the 1940's enabled scientists for the first time to quantify information. Because of his pioneering insight, a link between information and energy was revealed through the principle of entropy. For many scientists, Shannon's discovery was the equivalent of waking up and finding a marble on their doorstep. His theorem had enormous implications. It meant the ice melting in your glass could be precisely measured against the news coming from your TV, or a black hole swallowing a galaxy, or even the information encoded in our DNA.

But more than a quantitative tool, without which science can hardly be called "science," Shannon's thought opened a window on a strikingly new possibility: The idea that information resided at the most fundamental level of matter, and may in fact form the basis of the entire scheme.

"It from bit," is how John Wheeler, a renowned physicist and long-time Princeton resident, described the relationship, going so far as to say that, with respect to all things physical, we live in a "participatory universe." Were he around today, Tanhuma bar Abba, a Talmudic sage from the 4th century, would probably agree. "God reveals himself bit by bit," he is believed to have said.

Although few physicists, including Wheeler, would dare claim that God was part of the equation, "bit by bit" is the refrain now heard across the quantum world, from MIT to Cal Tech, as quantum programmers pursue the latest alchemical dream of subjugating the tiniest constituents of matter to serve as microprocessors.

It is not out of the question, then, to claim that we live in a crackling universe in communication with itself and with us. Indeed, the tip, tip, tap of information is all around. Like Morse code; like corn popping in a pan; like children lightly dancing on bubble wrap; like a marble tumbling in a clothes dryer. While we typically associate God and heavenly realms with light, sound is an analogue. Sound can encode the same information. God, it is said, *spoke* the world into existence. The sound of the Buddha's teaching, it is said, is everywhere. The birds, the trees, the sky, all echo the Dharma.

Regarding Shannon's work, however, one vital element was missing from his equation. The question humanity has been asking since consciousness arrived on the scene. What does it all *mean*?

Technology can convey information at light speed, over enormous distances, with negligible loss in transmission. But so far science cannot account for meaning. There are no scales or tools to determine its levels, as there are, say, for speed, temperature or pressure. Science cannot define meaning or quantify it. Meaning does not fit neatly into any formula. It is analogous to biologists who haven't yet provided an agreed-upon definition of "life." Yet, in our own lives, we all would profess to have the capacity to make such distinctions, and based on how we think or feel, reserve the right to decide for ourselves what's meaningful or not.

As a Creative Director employed in an advertising agency, I would never have drawn a parallel between my work and the heady world of quantum mechanics, but with information now being touted as the *sine qua non* of matter, accept it or not, here was a mutual source. And having worked with the biggest brands in America for nearly two decades, I knew something about the craft of attaching meaning to a slew of various inanimate objects, as well as intangible qualities and services.

Indeed, that was my job—to strategically carve out a message or two that would resound with relevance and vitality and rise above the din. It's no small feat to make it work. Many nuances are folded into the process. Far more than most people know. And such efforts are far less successful than most people think. That is why, from the standpoint of effective communications, I had to admire the universe! Frank's marble "pitch" was more convincing than any single communication I had ever seen or created.

And as I began to unravel it, the message—residing in a bead of glass, made of the same silicone compound in computer chips and optical fibers—seemed too weighty. Too much to cap and reserve for a few friends and myself, and entirely unsuited for the medium in which I was expert—the glib prose of commercial speak. The sound byte. In other words, language designed for people for whom the length of a fortune cookie is about as much as they can handle in one sitting.

"But we're not meant to keep these things to ourselves," a friend of mine assured me over a cup of coffee, urging me to bring this story to a wider audience. "We're *supposed* to share it."

"Hmmm," I thought to myself, "easy for you to say."

But the suggestion touched a nerve.

Could I be so bold, or crazy, as to give up a lucrative career to write a book about people finding marbles? About a guy who sets up a wacky, ad hoc experiment with his recently departed hairdresser friend and thinks he's found irrefutable evidence of God?

Utility theory demands that you examine your options as objectively as possible and make choices that will maximize your return. But what was my expected return? Nothing whatsoever, as far as I could tell. At the least, however, I could face myself in the morning. Because if all of this were true, and indeed, is true, how cowardly it would be to shrink before God.

I'm thinking about all this as I pace my office. My career in advertising spans nearly twenty years. I have been a good corporate citizen. Wait, I am being modest, a stellar corporate citizen. I have helped my agency win millions of dollars in business; assembled a dedicated and talented staff. Our clients are happy. My colleagues are happy. The firm's president, especially happy. But am I ready to trade it all in—my career, salary, bonus, benefits, risk whatever financial security I have—and for what? To chase a marble down a noisy street?

What could I possibly gain? And what would I tell Richard, the president? Or Anne, my girlfriend? Before I could broach the subject with any of them, there were more marble surprises in store. And I was feeling challenged enough with the ones already on the table.

CHAPTER 5

Carve your name on your heart and not on marble.
— Message in a Fortune Cookie

As Gwen noted in her email, a pattern was developing: the Sunday marble find. Sure enough, on the following Sunday, one week after Frank's death, two more marbles turned up out of the blue.

At around 6:30, Sunday evening, August 31st, I was visiting a friend, Manuel, in Newtown, Pennsylvania. His wife, Rachel, was out shopping. They had just moved into their new house over the weekend. But sadly their happiness had taken a heavy hit a few days earlier. Rachel was diagnosed with thyroid cancer and would need surgery.

Manuel was giving me the grand tour of his new

place. We were in his basement, on a newly cleaned rug that was just rolled out on a floor he had washed himself. We both had occasion to glance at the ground and noticed a marble resting directly beneath us. We were standing right over it. Manuel picked it up. "I believe this is for you," he said, presenting it to me as if it were a gift, clearly as surprised as I was with its sudden appearance.

"Are you kidding me?" I said.

I took the marble from Manuel's hand and recognized how similar it was to the one Gwen found in Minnesota. Manuel and I looked at each other. We were close workmates. We'd known each other for years. He knew the story about Frank's marble because I told him when I returned to work the day after Frank's funeral. Manuel was at a complete loss to explain how the marble suddenly appeared beneath us. The idea that he would plant it, or present it through some sleight-of-hand, was out of the question. I know his character. He is far too respectful to even consider, let alone stage, such a ploy. And besides, with Rachel's diagnosis, Manuel had more important things on his mind.

That Sunday was a workday for me, as it is for most workaholics. But now I felt like my job was calling me like a train whistle back to the mine. In fact, every moment since Jean's discovery, I felt myself closer to moving on in my life. Something shifted. I wasn't the same person I was before. Everything felt incidental to some larger operative principle. The little marble was making a mockery of my attachments.

In the past, if work left little room for a personal

life, I took it in stride. I focused on my career and completely sidestepped the idea of starting a family. It didn't matter all that much to me because the model seemed utterly flawed anyway. Still, while I had achieved immunity with respect to the trade-off between work and family, I could see the enormous toll my career had exacted on my life. My time was someone else's.

Leaving Manuel's house, I saw Rachel approaching. "Look what Manuel and I just found," I said, holding up the marble.

"Wow," said Rachel. "I found one, too!"

"Let me see," I asked. I was as surprised as Rachel and wondered why Manuel hadn't said anything. Rachel's marble was a deep blue. I had a feeling what it meant right away.

"It's a healing marble! Frank sent you a healing marble!"

My comment caught us both by surprise, but it was spontaneous. And though I felt exposed and awkward for speaking so soon, I knew what it was. I instantly connected Rachel's blue marble with images of the sky-blue Medicine Buddha's I'd seen, a source of healing for any physical ill.

Rachel looked confused and a bit startled.

"Didn't Manuel tell you?" I inquired.

"Tell me what?"

"The story, the marble story."

With so much going on in their lives, Manuel had not had a chance to share the story with Rachel. Neither was he aware that Rachel had found a marble earlier in the day, which, she said, seemed to roll out of nowhere, landing at her feet on her way into the laundry room. Although she was curious, she had no context for it. She picked it up and put it in her pocket, more relieved that Michelle, her two and a half year old daughter, had not found and swallowed it than anything else.

"Wait a second," I told Rachel, and walked over to my car. For some reason I had brought along a copy of a letter I sent to some friends detailing the marble story up to Gwen's discovery. As I was driving to their house, I wondered what impelled me to bring it. But now, seeing Rachel's surprise, the reason was clear. I had brought the letter for her. She needed to read it.

"Take a look at this," I said. "It will explain everything." I added, "Don't worry, you're going to be okay."

I spoke with Rachel the next day after she read my letter. She said she felt much calmer about her health crisis and the surgery she was facing.

"Why?" I asked her.

"Because I can feel the love in it," she said. "When I realized what I had, I knew everything was going to be fine."

Rachel's words made it all sound simple and beautiful. She decoded the message: love, hope, and healing. Still nursing the wounds of my childhood after so many years, I had to admit I could use some of that myself. I sent Gwen the following email that Sunday evening when I returned home with the marble from Manuel's house:

From: Michael
Date: Sun, 31 Aug 2003 22:40:38 -0400

To: Gwen
Subject: Another one, like yours

Yes, Frank, we got the message. Loud and clear.

With utter certainty, you have made the spiritual dimension come alive for us with a level of intensity and immediacy we have never known. And you have brought humor, finesse, and style to your demonstration, as well as shown your infinite ability to orchestrate, near and far, using the channels of love and friendship and trust. So tonight, Gwen, just an hour ago, yes, this very Sunday evening, when I was visiting my friend Manuel in his new house that he and his family just moved into. A house with floors newly mopped and rugs cleaned, what do you suppose my friend Manuel scooped up off the floor right in front of us, that he swears was not there before, and wonders himself how it ever got there?

Yes, a marble. Like yours.
Love,
Michael

Because Gwen and I shared a similar background, and because our marbles looked alike, we dubbed ourselves, the "Marble Twins." That connection runs deeper than it sounds.

Gwen was one of the few people I could speak openly to about my abusive past. She had experienced something similar. She was a survivor. She understood the tripping-out, light-years-away, dissociative state, and how hard the return journey could be. Together we spoke a different language, like two exiles from the same hellish land who made it to safer shore. We needed only a few words, a few sighs and gestures, to convey to each other what we experienced.

Gwen was further along in her healing and was writing a book about her experience. I admired her for that. I couldn't imagine going public with my own story. But that presented a dilemma. Could I tell the marble story without revealing the most painful parts of my life? In that case, where would the meaning reside, in outrageous possibility alone?

It is more difficult to confess to my vulnerability than attempt to describe the ineffable. Who wants to expose their wounds, or reveal their weaknesses? The marble lifted my emotional state. There was no question about that. It signified something greater. To exclude the healing aspect would be to deny the love Frank was offering. Most victims of child abuse suffer a kind of living death. But Frank was demonstrating no trauma is final or insurmountable. It was a virtuosic performance, to say the least. And I was not the only spectator with a front-row seat. This was theater in the round. All were welcome. I had the ridiculous urge to get to the bottom of it, as if understanding how it works could make it all work better, or that a simple explanation was in the offing.

I decided to take the marble I retrieved at Manuel's house on a little fact-finding trip and meet with my friend Rinchen in New York.

Rinchen headed up the largest humanitarian

organization serving Tibet. For many years he was also the Dalai Lama's chief representative in North America. Over a cup of coffee, I showed Rinchen the marble I retrieved at Manuel's house and shared its provenance. Like an expert on "Antique Roadshow," he picked it up, rolled it around in his hands and then held it up to the light.

"Bava was a Tulku," Rinchen stated, without hesitation.

"What is a Tulku?" I asked.

"A Tulku is an enlightened being who may choose the manner of his rebirth."

That Rinchen elevated Frank to something approaching saintly status, based solely on my evidence and a few of Frank's marble-manifesting feats, did not surprise me. There were times when Frank and I were together that he seemed more like St. Francis than just plain Frank. Birds of all kinds flocked to his backyard. Frank would place a few seeds in his palm and within minutes a bird would swoop down and rest on his forefinger, and from that perch, calmly peck at some choice morsel, while other birds would patiently wait on Frank's head or shoulder to have their turn.

What also impressed me about Rinchen's response was the no-frills way he talked about Frank, and how the occurrence of something that most of us would describe as extraordinary was an accepted part of his reality. It seemed an expansive way to embrace life.

I thanked Rinchen then headed cross-town to catch my train.

Over the next few days I considered what Rinchen had to say. But since I'm not someone who automatically accepts the words of anyone, I decided to do some further investigation, which led to a slight revision of Rinchen's assessment.

I believe Frank was a Tulku, as Rinchen stated. But that he was also a Terton, a uniquely American version. If there was never such a being on our Western shores, now there was, in the person of Frank Bava.

In the Nyingma tradition of Tibetan Buddhism, Tertons are recognized as finders of hidden treasures. They are considered emanations, or incarnations, of the great Padmasambhava himself.

Padmasambhava was said to have placed hidden treasures in the ground to be discovered at a later time, when humankind was ready to receive such information that could further its advancement. This information could take any form, concealed as earth, stones, trees or sky, depending on the nature and capabilities of the receiver.

Tertons had rank. The highest were considered "Mad Finders" of the chief treasures. They could not be attached to property or things, only spiritual pursuits. Interesting enough, tradition says most Tertons came from the ranks of ordinary people. Their natural directness and honesty could be an affront to others. It was their inner spiritual attainments that made them special.

Frank, aka Bava-Sambhava to his best friends, clearly belonged to the "Mad Finders" category. And I have it on scholarly authority that a Terton is assumed to be a Tulku, but not necessarily the other way around.

During this period I continued to go to work and consult with a psychotherapist. I was still suffering from PTSD and realized, following that diagnosis, that I had been dealing with it my entire life. Fortunately, my therapist was trained as a Jungian analyst. Why fortunately? With respect to the marbles, which I dragged into therapy like someone might bring their spouse, she had a context for the *numinous*. Coined by Rudolf Otto, a German theologian, numinous is a word for moments and objects that have the power to transform.

Jungians love that word. For Carl Jung, the famous Swiss psychologist and contemporary of Freud, there could be no deep emotional healing without an awareness and acceptance of our larger self. Our Divine Self, if you will. For that to occur, some catalyst is needed. That spark is the numinous event. What does this have to do with the marbles in this story? Everything, or perhaps more accurately, almost everything. Because in Jung's scheme the roadmap to healing and transformation starts at the signpost of Wholeness. That is its numinosity. And that could be any one of a thousand things, with the only requirement that it lift you beyond yourself because of its majesty, its beauty. And along with that, an aura of sacredness, or as Jung put it, a transcendent quality. It will touch your heart and soul like nothing before, and move you from hither to yon, and in so doing establish the coordinates of a greater consciousness.

As far as I'm concerned, the marble could indeed qualify as a poster child for wholeness. But the real numinous experience occurred when I first learned of Jean's discovery. That was the turning point. The moment that lifted me out of myself, when I was instantly struck by the feeling that Frank had served up the marble with God's assistance. That sense is what blew the doors off its hinges in my tidy little view of how the world works.

"That's all well and good," someone might concede. Marbles may well be the stuff Jungian dreams are made of. But how does one's personal numinous object become numinous for so many?

Jung had an answer for that, too. He called it the "participation mystique," a term he credited to Lucien Levy-Bruhl, a French anthropologist. This phenomenon is similar in dynamic to the solo rendition, except it touches a shared, or what Jung called "collective," layer of unconscious. Thus, it may affect others, a great many others.

Let us understand that in Jung's view the numinosity perceived in or from the object in question must ultimately be superseded by the realization of our divine wholeness, which lies within, if it is to become an important factor in healing. So, while Jung's analysis may initially serve to strip away the numinous quality of the object or experience, leaving it denuded, so to speak, of its sublime power, that energy is transferred to its rightful place, the larger reality of one's greater nature.

I could not argue with Jung's insight, assuming I understood it correctly. Much of it made sense. I stood ready to denude my marble of any numinosity. Crush it in a vice. Or flush it down the toilet for all I cared. But where this story is concerned, there seemed to be an important piece missing. Rather, a person missing. And that, of course, was Frank.

Someone who has a numinous encounter is bound to feel that his or her own experience smells sweeter than someone else's. That's human nature. But surely when there is clear evidence that when a second party existing outside the physical realm wants to join in on the fun, and similar events ensue, that is not your garden variety sunset, or whatever may serve to deeply inspire, however beautiful it might be. Multiple events, seemingly propelled by the same force (i.e. Frank) all pointed to other, transpersonal phenomena beyond merely that of a personal, one-and-done, numinous event.

So the Jungian perspective helped lighten my load. It explained the palpable sense of movement to a greater center. But there still seemed quite a bit of unfinished business. Not the least of which was that a new current was sweeping me further away from the narrow confines of my job.

Another Sunday was approaching, and by Gwen's reckoning another marble should be headed our way. I waited for word. I began keeping notes, tracking the story. I was the scribe of a small but growing group of "marble holders," which included Jean, Gwen, Rachel, and me. All of us felt blessed. Once the characteristic element of a child's game, each marble was now a point through which we could feel Frank's presence as he continued to tap out a unique code. Admittedly, I had yet to succeed in denuding my marble of its numinosity. Or as one of my clever friends dubbed it, given its powerful charisma, its "Paul Newmanosity," the fellow who now smiles back at us from soup-can labels, salad dressing bottles, and popcorn about to pop in a participatory universe.

CHAPTER 6

Unutterable is the wonder of Thy Sport
— The Gurū Granth Sāhib

Paula, the owner of the salon where Frank worked, knew nothing of the marble story the Sunday afternoon she drove to pick up Vincent, her nine-year old son, at his nanny's house on the other side of Queens from where Frank lived.

"Look," Vincent said to Paula, proudly holding up a big mesh bag as he stepped into her car. "Nanny gave me 102 marbles!"

"What are you doing with those?" Paula asked. She had never seen Vincent display any interest in marbles before.

Vincent was playing in his nanny's house when a part to his toy rolled under a table. He went to retrieve the part and found two big bags of marbles hidden under the table. Delighted with his discovery, he asked his nanny if he could have them. She could only part with one bag, telling Vincent how much she enjoyed playing marbles when she was his age. Then she spent the rest of the morning teaching him how to play.

But why "102 marbles?" I wondered. Did that number have some special significance? Was some additional meaning being conveyed?

The number 102, I later discovered, is considered a "harshad" number, defined as being divisible by the sum of its digits. The name is taken from Sanskrit, a combination of *harsa* (joy) and *da* (giving). With his gift of 102 marbles, Frank was bringing joy to Vincent, who, returning home later that afternoon, couldn't wait to play marbles with his friends in the neighborhood. And he'd already become something of an expert through the coaching of his nanny.

For Meher Baba, the Guru who in the 1960s gave the Boomer generation the expression "Don't worry. Be happy," playing marbles not only brought him joy, it was a game with "deep significance." A game played by "seers" and "sages" in what he called a "divine sport of consciousness," before final Realization is achieved. "Since the beginning of time," he claimed, "I have been playing marbles with the universe."

While Frank and I could hardly claim such a sustained record of marble playing, it was certainly curious to find an Avatar such as Meher Baba extolling the game. And he was not alone in recognizing the significance of play.

Arthur M. Young, a brilliant inventor and writer

of *The Reflexive Universe*, built his theory on evolutionary process with the firm belief that play is more than a primary force. It is a "fundamental entity," he said, the "first cause." It is "more basic than the fundamental particles it can create."

The Bible doesn't say, "*Before* the beginning, God thought, 'Let's Play!'" But it is an intriguing idea. Imagine yourself utterly alone. You are infinite eternal space. Wouldn't You long for someone to play with? And then, Presto! The world comes into existence because You want to play. You had to leave Your playmates a little free will, i.e. give up a tiny bit of control (which You could kibosh at any moment), or the game would be too predictable. With that came time, and the need to monitor it, essentially a play clock.

Albert Einstein is claimed to have said he wanted to know God's thoughts. But he never accepted indeterminacy as part of the equation. So he would never have agreed with Young. In another famous remark, Einstein said, "God doesn't play dice." But in this instance, he was wrong. Play abounds. All the fellows Einstein was consorting with in his day proved that chance is as entrenched as gravity.

When I phoned Paula to learn about Vincent's marbles, she didn't sound in the mood to play, but she tried to be a good sport all the same.

"Hi Michael, I heard you and Frank have been having a good time—with marbles. Jean told me the other day when she was in for a cut."

"That's true," I said. "And I heard from Jean that Vincent's come into a few himself. That's why I'm calling."

"Yes," Paula admitted, "102 to be exact. Which he's fond of telling everyone."

Vincent suddenly grabbed the line, sounding far more animated than Paula.

"There're 102," Vincent confirmed. "I counted every one."

"Do you like playing with them?"

"Yes," he admitted. "But I also like chess."

"So do I," I said, and recalled the last time I looked at a chessboard, when Frank's marble was bouncing in the drier.

"Did you know a lot of Frank's friends are finding marbles, like you?"

"Yes, my mom told me. It's amazing!"

When Paula got back on the line she communicated the same benevolent skepticism she typically extended Frank when he was working in her salon. That annoyed me.

"One day," I told Paula, "visitors who have heard the miraculous story about Frank and the marbles will seek your shop in Soho. They will want to see where Frank stood, cutting hair, dreaming of wild woods in Maine. Feeling God's hands on his shoulder as he smiled in the mirror." And I said this with absolute certainty.

"Sure," Paula said. "I'll believe it when I see it."

So we made a bet. Planted with the right intention, and given the right conditions, seeds grow, and inspired teachers and healers emerge from the mist when we need them. That is not fable, but fact.

Leah, another colleague of mine, never met Frank. She had no reason to make an absurd wager with me on whether onlookers would one day gather outside Paula's storefront window, or that Frank's bio might wind up in some modern hagiography. Neither was she in a playful mood when Monday, September 22nd rolled around; she was downright stressed.

That morning, Leah was required to stop taking her blood-thinning medication. It was the first major test of her surgery. A few months earlier, a device was implanted in her heart to seal the congenital hole that was discovered in a routine examination.

Leah woke up earlier than usual. She swung her legs around, and stepping on a white rug beside her bed, was "freaked" to find a small round object beneath her foot. She picked it up and stared at the smooth emerald green stone, the size of a marble.

"My God, how did *this* get here?" she wondered.

The day before her house had been completely cleaned. The white rug in her bedroom was vacuumed and spotless. There was only one explanation: Frank.

Leah learned about Frank from me a few days earlier when I told her about the marbles.

"This is for you," she said, rather abruptly, holding out her hand when we were coming out of a meeting.

I picked up the stone and smiled.

"No," I said to Leah, looking over the beautiful green stone. "It's for you," handing it back.

I sensed Leah's reluctance to accept it from the start. Her feigned indifference at the miraculous nature of her discovery didn't fool me. You can't disown such a gift so casually. Still, I knew exactly what she was struggling with. Most of us are more accustomed to putting up with difficulties rather than accepting blessings.

And then there is the burden of debt. "If I accept this" goes the argument, "how can I repay it? What is my obligation?"

Such things are never stated outright. But I could tell because I was thinking the same thing. And I was amused at Leah's desire to relinquish her gift, to free herself of the burden. But it was too late. She had already accepted the message it contained.

"Yes," she had to admit, holding the stone a little tighter in her hand when I returned it. "It has brought me some calm, once I got over its freaky appearance under my foot! I'm going off my blood thinners," she explained. "This is going to be a risky time for me."

Two months later Leah learned that not only was her surgery successful, she was also pregnant. She felt doubly relieved. Her doctor said she would be healthy enough to carry the baby without endangering her own life or her child's.

Still, despite all the good news, Leah's reluctance was crying out for further assurance. That would come a few months later in a manner that would leave no doubt.

Leah's stone reminded me of Frank's marble because of its organic quality. As I shared, Frank's marble could easily have passed for a polished stone. We were never quite sure.

I was also struck by how Leah found it. Because the day before, I had occasion to share the marble phenomenon with Richard, the president of the agency I worked for, when we were traveling to New York. The next morning he told me, "I was sure I was going to wake up and step on a marble." But it was Leah, not

Richard, who was the beneficiary of his prediction.

I had come to realize that while our marbles were conveyed in an incomprehensible manner, the addressee was clearly written on them, so there was no doubt for whom they were meant, even if it took a day or two to sort it out. Each marble—or in Leah's case, small stone—had purpose and direction. I flashed on the entire apparatus. It was nature's network, with Frank near or at the hub.

In technical terms, the marbles as information were being routed through a complex communications net with nodes, queues, and delays, addressed to a specific receiver capable of understanding its meaning.

For example, after Jean found her marble at the entrance to her home in Brooklyn, Gwen and Amelia both asked me whether I was going to ask Jean for the marble. After all, it was I who asked Frank to "toss it back." Jean needed only turn the marble over to me and the mission would be completed.

My answer was always "No." Something told me that the marble was meant for Jean. That is how Jean felt about it, too. On the other hand, when Gwen told her story in Minnesota, she came home with the marble in her pocket because there was no mistaking to whom it belonged. Again, although Manuel and I were standing together in his house when he bent down and picked up the marble, his immediate instinct was to present it to me.

On yet another Sunday afternoon, a few weeks out from Leah's discovery, another marble arrived special delivery for Gigi, a friend of mine who lives in Sarasota, Florida. It didn't matter that Gigi wasn't there to accept it at that moment. It was axiomatic that it would eventually find her.

Gigi knew Frank and learned about the marble story from me early in its development. But she hadn't shared the story with any of her associates at the bookstore she managed, nor did she feel any reason to. That is why nobody paid much attention to the Graying Man who casually entered the store on a Sunday afternoon, briefly looked around, then walked up to the cashier and delivered from his pocket a marble. "This is for you," he said, sweetly. Then he just as quickly walked out.

The cashier thought the incident odd, to say the least, and placed the marble on the counter. The next day Gigi came to work and noticed the marble. It was intended for her, she just didn't realize it yet. She looked at the marble periodically throughout the day. "We were almost flirting with each other," she said.

Gigi left that evening with the marble still on the counter, and on her mind. She didn't return to work until after the following day, when she noticed the marble was gone. Curious, she inquired about it. She asked the storeowner, Kelly, if she'd seen the marble.

"Yes," Kelly said. "It was beautiful. No one claimed it, so I told Donna she could have it." Then Gigi told Kelly the marble story. "Oh," Kelly said, "it must be for you."

Then Gigi went to Donna, "Do you have the marble?"

"No," Donna said. "Davvy collects marbles and loved it, so I gave it to her."

Gigi then told Donna the marble story.

"Oh," Donna said, "it must be for you."

Gigi found Davvy. "Do you still have the marble you got from Donna?"

"Yes," Davvy said.

"May I see it?" Gigi asked.

Davvy had taken it home. And now, for the third time that day, Gigi shared the marble story. "Oh," Davvy said, "it must be for you. I'll bring it with me tomorrow." The next day she gave Gigi the marble.

On my phone Wednesday evening there was a brief message from Gigi. "Dude, I have a marble!"

When I called Gigi back, she said the shift in her awareness was unmistakable. The evening she took her marble home, she slept with it under her pillow. And now she wears it in a small pouch around her neck so it is with her all the time. "Since I was gifted the marble," she told me, "my whole being feels upgraded. I feel more compassionate. I feel I'm operating from another place."

CHAPTER 7

Ohhhh Lucy!
— Ricky Ricardo

I loved Anne very much. But she always seemed drawn to the best thing that was the worst thing for our relationship. Her actions showed little regard for herself as well. You could say she had a knack for both self, and joint, sabotage.

She revealed to me when we first started going out that she chose her first husband with less consideration than she gave the qualities of a new dress. Of course I thought that was peculiar. Who in their right mind wouldn't? The possible shelf life of a husband would seem to demand at least as much attention to detail as one might employ in choosing an article of clothing.

Still, her admission at the time did not completely

alarm me. I liked Anne's honesty. It explained her appreciation for fashion. And there was some humor in her observation. So I gave her the benefit of the doubt. I assumed she had developed enough self-awareness since her first marriage not to make the same mistake twice. That was a mistake on my part.

We met one afternoon when I was on a business trip. She was sitting across from me in a conference room in Minnesota, and I fell in love with her instantly. The present never looked so beautiful. It was almost a Paul Numinosity moment. And the feeling, I would shortly learn, was mutual.

But a boundary needed to be crossed. Anne was a client. She ran one of the accounts my agency worked on. It's never a good idea to get involved with a client. Everyone knows that. But that didn't stop us from flying into each other's arms at the first opportunity.

The way Anne carried herself enchanted me, and the loving manner in which she held her children close to her heart, wrapping them in her long, beautiful hands, as if Modigliani had sketched a Madonna.

Anne was separated from her second husband. Yes, she claimed, she obviously made another bad decision. This time I cringed when she tried explaining it... something about her emotional weakness at that period in her life...pressure from her family...her intended's attractive crop of blonde hair...reminding her of Björn Borg, the Swedish tennis star of the 1970s.

"Good grief," I wondered, "what have I gotten into?"

One day, searching through Anne's garbage when she was at work, Björn (let us call him that) found her phone records, which included her calls to me. The next thing I knew I was receiving threatening messages from Björn in Minnesota.

Imagine a Swede trying to act like Joe Pesci in *Good Fellas*. This was not the Minnesota I knew from *Prairie Home Companion*. Björn sounded like he had every intention of driving to Pennsylvania with a semi-automatic. And he was more relentless in threatening Anne.

Orders of protection were filed. But now our relationship was under a cloud in the form of a big, husky, abusive ice-fisherman. When Björn had the audacity to call my workplace and leave threatening messages on my voicemail, I thought it best to speak with Richard, the man in the corner office, and reveal the unvarnished truth: that I was seeing a client and her crazed soon-to-be ex-husband was calling the agency.

Anne and Björn's break-up began when he opted to go on a hunting trip rather than remain by her side while she was recovering from a life-threatening hemorrhage after the birth of their son. That was the turning point for Anne, when she told her husband not to come back.

She described that day to me, her lying in the hospital, blood oozing out of her, staining the sheets red, as Björn headed out the door because he didn't want to miss the start of deer season. Hunting was more important to him than staying with Anne, while she remained in serious condition.

"Why do you look so sad?" I once asked her. I wanted to make her happy more than anyone I'd ever met.

She started crying as she told me her story. She was three when her mother ran off with a salesman. She was raised by her father, an engineer. He was an austere man who had no qualms about pulling her pants down in front of guests and whipping her backside with a belt.

I realized why my heart went out to her. Anne was a kindred soul. But sadness and victimhood was not the place I wanted to live anymore. I was seeking professional help and facing the ghosts that were haunting me. Anne deferred such help, claiming she had no time for it.

Every workplace is a bit of a soap opera, with cheesy plot lines and bad dialogue. But the story is not all that amusing when it's your own, and when it potentially impacts a large piece of business. I wasn't sure what Richard was going to say when, taking a seat in his office, I transformed it into a confessional. There was no whispering or latticework between us, just a wide expanse of executive desk, from where Richard could sense I was disturbed about something.

"Everything okay?"

"Not exactly," I admitted.

"You're not ill, I hope?"

"Oh no," I said, "nothing like that."

And then I unpacked the story like it was a big box of Legos from the Mall of America, taking full responsibility for the whole embarrassing predicament.

"We met there," I said, "she said that...he did this...and now her crazy husband who Anne is separated from is calling here, saying he wants to use me as bait on his next ice-fishing trip."

Richard slowly digested my tale of love and lust bordering on professional misconduct. I forget his exact words. But to my great relief he seemed more concerned with how I was feeling than any potential impact on the business.

"And how do you feel about Anne?" he asked.

"I love her," I said.

"Tell her I said hello the next time you see her."

And that was that. Richard was a good man.

So corporate life continued virtually unchanged for me, except for the marbles. The continued emergence of these objects would soon lead to yet another and final act of penance in Richard's office. Only this time I wouldn't need forgiveness for the error of my ways. I was getting ready to resign, and still struggling with the notion that I might regret it later.

In Judaism, I learned, there is a stage in one's spiritual evolution when sheer determination will not help. A gift or favor must be granted to get beyond that point, a blessing that takes one's faith to a new level.

Descartes, on the other hand, viewed God as innate. A conclusion he drew not from faith, but logic. As brilliant as Descartes was, however, his deduction was nothing new. Four thousand years or so before him, a man named Abraham, with nothing more than his own critical faculties, reasoned there must be some great indivisible force in the world: a Creator, a God. It was only after Abraham steadfastly stuck to his own logical conviction that God spoke to him.

It took the Catholic Church a bit longer, two thousand years or so, to officially approve the same methodology Abraham used to reach his conclusion.

In 1870, the Vatican Council decreed that God could be known, "by the natural powers of human reason."

As wonderful as miracles are to behold, or revelations are to experience, there are disadvantages, not the least of which is that not everyone can be present to either witness the former, or believe what their eyes are telling them; nor are they predisposed to experiencing the latter. So the Vatican Council was a vote of confidence for human reason. It made it official. It's okay to circumvent your heart and discover the truth of the divine by way of your brain.

If God can be logically deduced, and satisfy the calculations of countless individuals throughout history, why does the reality of His/Her/Its existence need to be gifted? Perhaps the simple answer is that we all have different capacities. Some arrive logically; some intuitively. Some are swayed by the touch of a peacock's feather. Some need to be whacked on the head. And some of us never get there.

In ancient Greece, a traveler might come upon a heap of stones in his wanderings and ascribe this lucky find to the grace of God. It was called a *hermaion*. Such was Frank Bava's gift for me, a handful of marbles that mark a new boundary beyond which greater understanding resides.

But inevitably, try as we will, the miraculous becomes integrated into the routine. The blessings for which we are thankful, or the logic we employed to arrive at some transformative truth, are quickly forgotten. In those instances, the universe is still accommodating and seems to await our return. There are other moments, however, when patience seems to be lacking, and we may be summoned loudly, and not all that benignly, as I was to learn. Either way, once we have acquired the requisite vision, but through our indifference begin to take for granted how infinitely vast and supportive It is, something may appear to remind us of the greater mystery to which we are all connected.

That is exactly what happened to Nicole as she took a seat on the #165 Paramus bus from New York City to Oradell, New Jersey.

"Oh my God!" Nicole exclaimed. "There's a marble!" It was sitting right next to her.

"At first I was freaked," Nicole explained. "Then I felt honored, and happy. Frank and I were friends. He was confirming that our friendship mattered."

Nicole learned of Frank's death when she called the salon to schedule an appointment. That's when she heard about the marble story. On her return trip from New York that Sunday afternoon there were plenty of seats on the bus. She took one without giving it much thought. Then she noticed the marble resting right next to her, a blue, pink, and teal marble that she now carries everywhere.

I heard about Nicole's marble through Gwen. As soon as I got Nicole's number, I left a message on her work phone to please call me. The timing was interesting. Just after Nicole listened to my message, Fran, a co-worker of Nicole's, stopped by her desk.

"Look what I found," Fran said, holding up some pennies she found in the street.

Fran's statement didn't register with Nicole.

"You mean you don't know? Every time you find a penny," Fran explained, "someone who has passed is saying 'hello.'"

"Reeeeeally?" said Nicole. "I think you should listen to *this*." Nicole played my message about wanting to talk to her about Frank and the marble she found on the bus.

I laughed when Nicole relayed all this to me. She had no way of knowing how her exchange with Fran paralleled my experience with Amelia. In the context of Nicole's find, Amelia's pennies were back, shining brightly. It was something I needed to learn. There is no hierarchy among signs. Amidst ubiquity are blessings we don't see, although I will admit it is difficult not to play favorites. For me, like Nicole, marbles will always trump pennies.

And then there's Akira's marble discovery.

Akira was a stylist who had worked with Frank. He was in Minnesota for a wedding. On a Sunday afternoon, his friend's family invited him to look at a house they were interested in buying. Akira agreed to go. But for reasons he can't explain, the owner of the house that was for sale took a special interest in him as soon as they arrived.

"If you wouldn't mind," the owner said, "could I show you something?"

Akira, being polite, obliged. The owner led him into his den...and the largest marble collection Akira had ever seen. Cases upon cases of rare marbles were placed before him: Latticinio swirls. Joseph coats. Banded lutzes. Peppermint swirls. Clambroths. Mists. Agates. Indians. Slags, Opaques and Clearies. Sulphides, Ribbon Lutzes and Onionskins. All represented and lovingly cared for in one enormous collection.

Akira spun in the room. "Frank is having a good laugh!" he shouted. "He is all around me having a good laugh!"

From the mid-1960s into the 1980s, chance was cool. Experimental musicians like John Cage and artists like Jackson Pollock splattered notes and color against their canvases, finding collaboration with the spirit of the moment. It was a celebration of a discontinuous world, one that physicists know isn't neat and tidy, but spins and jumps probabilistically, not deterministically.

Through training and technique, the artist takes control over his creation under the assumption that he has control. But what would happen to art, to life, if the balance shifted? What if chance threw the artist against the canvas? And the chef into the soup? Would we still call it chance? What kind of performance is it when we're not sure who is playing with whom? "Don't play the saxophone. Let the saxophone play you," Charlie Parker, the gifted jazzman, advised.

An English logician, G. Spencer-Brown, arrived on the scene at the burgeoning of the chance movement with a mathematical proof that few people understood at the time. He showed how the perceived universe will periodically reveal its Maker, and how, starting from unmarked space, the world is constructed in a way that allows It to know Itself. For Spencer-Brown, life is a journey of "re-discovery," of unlearning what we have been led to believe, and seizing what we already knew, in a perpetual game of "hide and seek."

Paradox is perhaps the most subtle and mystifying aspect of our condition. It is the ultimate pun. Play at its purest. Henry Horace Williams, four decades before Spencer-Brown, beautifully articulated the puzzling relationship that exists between the subjective and the objective, and the uncertainty of whether we are "constructing" or "discovering." He realized that the conscious and the unconscious must be accounted for, not dismissed because it might confound the math. And he boldly asserted that the first stage of knowledge is "a miracle." Pretty incredible stuff from a logician, if you ask me.

I am perhaps too enamored of people like Williams and Spencer-Brown, who solely on the strength of their mathematical ability can arrive at an exalted truth, while I have only a marble from Frank to light the way. Without that gift, I would have remained as ignorant as a lamppost.

CHAPTER 8

The truth shall spring up from the earth
— Psalms 85:11

Miles Featherstone is Lakota. He grew up on the Cheyenne River reservation in South Dakota in the late nineteen forties and early fifties. After a stint in the Navy, Miles landed in New York City and soon found himself on the police force where he became a detective.

Miles has a unique way of expressing himself. His delivery is at once deadpan and profound. Like the comedian Jack Benny, he is a master of pregnant pauses and one-liners, particularly as it relates to Western man. For Miles, Europeans are more funny than they are tragic. I could have told him that L.A. just broke off into the Pacific, and he might say, "Oh, really? I was wondering when they would get around to that." Besides knowing how to laugh, Miles is fearless.

One day on Sheridan Square, just off Seventh Avenue in New York City, a mugger was aiming a gun squarely at Miles' face.

"I wouldn't do that," Miles warned politely, sensing he was really going to shoot. What the mugger didn't know is that Miles was trained as a Navy Seal. And that his reflexes are nano-fast.

Miles' warning didn't stop the mugger—who pulled the trigger anyway. But Miles got his finger between the hammer and the barrel before the gun could fire. The mugger was cuffed and on the ground before he knew what had happened. Miles had a sore finger for weeks, which was a small price to pay when you consider the alternative.

Miles and I were good friends in Manhattan where I lived and worked years ago, when New York, specifically Madison Avenue, was the center of the advertising world. We frittered away many hours at his apartment on West End Avenue watching sci-fi movies from his extensive collection. When his mother, Loretta, became ill in the early nineties, Miles moved to Minneapolis to take care of her and begin a career in social services on behalf of the Native American community. He grew up exposed to the traditional values and language of the Lakota people—a culture that has not lost respect for this earth. The Lakota language points to this hallowed understanding.

About six months after Frank's death and the opening of the marble floodgates, I had the chance to get together with Miles on one of my trips to Minnesota to see Anne.

As we drove to dinner, I handed Miles a CD of Deep Forest's *Boheme*. He slipped the CD into the player and I directed him to the "Bava-sambhava" track. He took to the lush rhythms immediately. I was sharing some of the events that took place since Frank's death, when I noticed a smile on Miles' face.

"What is it?" I asked.

"I just found a marble," he said, "two, in fact."

"You're kidding," I said. But I knew he wasn't.

Miles relayed his experience of finding two marbles in the ground on a Sunday afternoon in late August of 2003, shortly after Frank died. He was tending a garden in the back of his house. He wasn't long into his weeding when he spotted a marble in a hole he had dug around a root. He picked up the marble and examined it. But, as Miles explained, it wasn't until he found a second marble, a steely, just underneath the first, that sparked his reverie.

"For all I know it could have been an hour," Miles said. It was the combination of the steely, a shooter marble made of steel, along with the other glass marble he found, that unlocked a memory of knuckling down on the hard ground in South Dakota with his cousin, Jerald. The Lakota reservation in the forties and fifties was a harsh place to live. "But those moments," Miles said, "playing marbles with my cousin, was more than pleasant. It was perfect." And then he added, switching to another time frame, "I realized everything was going to be okay."

"What do you mean, okay?" I asked

"My cousin, Jerald, committed suicide a few

months ago," Miles informed me. "I was thinking about him. Now I knew he was at peace."

It took a long Minnesota winter before Miles was able to make his way to the shed in the back of his house to retrieve the marbles he had stored in the pocket of his garden cart. They had become something more than just marbles. They had become sacred.

Wakan in Lakota means sacred or holy. And *Yuwakan* refers to a transformation to a state of sacredness. A blessing, then, is that which transforms the profane into the sacred. Here was the marble story wrapped in one beautiful Lakota word, *Yuwakan*. All this was revealed in a book called *Sacred Language* by William Powers, which I had purchased years before because of my friendship with Miles.

Another interesting passage in Powers' book caught my attention. He talks about being presented with a gift by a tribal leader, Plenty Wolf. It was a tiny transparent stone found near an anthill in the Badlands.

Writes Powers: "The stones, roots, insects and the earth itself that are located underground are considered purer than the surface because they have not been contaminated by people or animals that live above. Stones that are pushed up by ants and other creatures are particularly sacred and are the ones selected for use in rituals."

Like Plenty Wolf's stone, Frank found his marble pushed up from the earth in my crawl space. And he, too, immediately accepted its sacredness.

The idea of a sacred stone was rolling across many spiritual traditions, and I was intent to follow it. I asked

Miles if he knew a Lakota elder, someone respected in the community, who could meet with us and share his feelings about our experience. Miles knew such an elder, a man I will call "James" in respect for his privacy. James teaches the Lakota language and follows a traditional path. Before we could meet, however, there was something I needed to do.

"Get some natural tobacco," Miles instructed me. "Make an offering of it in the place where Frank found his marble, then bring the pouch of tobacco with you when we meet with James."

The morning before I left for Minnesota to meet the elder, I went downstairs to my basement and pushed the ladder against the stone wall where there was an opening into the crawl space. With a flashlight in one hand and a bag of tobacco in my back pocket, I made my way over the red Pennsylvania dirt to the old cistern. As Miles instructed, I said a few prayers of thanks and sprinkled the tobacco over the very place where Frank had found his marble, a gift from the earth that was finally receiving acknowledgement.

But here is a secret I never told Frank. Nor anyone. Frank wasn't the first person to find the marble—I was.

Months before Frank's discovery, I'm not sure exactly how many, I was insulating a corner of my house and spotted the same crystal stone. It was sitting lightly in the dirt, only partially covered, just as Powers described. There was a slight gleam to it, as if it were backlit, as if a crack of light had opened beneath it. At the time, I didn't know what to make of it. I wondered what it was doing there, how had it gotten there. There was something about it that didn't feel comfortable. So instead of removing it, I pushed it deeper into the ground, as deep as I could. I was not ready to participate in whatever it represented.

And yet it emerged again. And when Frank saw it, he knew what he had found. He knew it was *Wakan,* sacred. And when he showed it to me, I was astounded. Because I recalled how deep I pushed it back into the ground. But I also felt sharing my prior discovery might diminish Frank's excitement. I saw no point in doing that. So I didn't tell Frank that I had already found it. Unlike me, Frank had the courage to accept it. He deserved it. And needless to say, had I removed it, or selfishly claimed title to it because it was on my property, this story would never have been written. As it turns out, my leaving it exactly where I found it was the right thing to do.

As Gwen pointed out when I revealed this, "So you tried to bury it twice: Once in the dirt in the crawl space. Once again with Frank at his funeral. And on both occasions, Frank brought it back to your awareness. How amazing is that?"

Then I realized what a great teacher Frank was. How many of us try to bury the best part of ourselves. Frank would not let that happen to me. What an incredible friend to bring this to my attention, and not to give up, until I got the message.

As I emerged from the crawl space, I sensed an important rendezvous with James, although it had not yet been confirmed.

Later that afternoon, I arrived in Minneapolis just a few hours ahead of the first winter's storm. Anne met me at the airport. We then drove six hours to the Boundary Waters in Northern Minnesota, a vast wilderness area with over a million acres and hundreds of lakes and rivers near Lake Superior. It offers just the kind of clean air and pristine vistas Frank used to dream about. In fact, he knew about this part of the world and talked about it with Anne whenever he saw her.

"I always knew Frank would have loved it here," she said. And in the two days we had to relax, I could see she was right. The Boundary Waters was hours out of cell phone distance, which would have been another compelling attraction for Frank. But when we were in range on our drive back, I heard from Miles that James was available to meet with us.

The following evening, Miles picked me up at Anne's house and we drove to St. Paul. Arriving a little early, we took a seat at a Perkins Restaurant where James had requested we meet and waited for him to join us. Miles and I ordered tea while he read over an early draft of this book. I also wanted to explore some of the details with James.

James arrived right on schedule and took a seat across from me. I felt close to him immediately. I sensed the feeling was mutual and expressed my thanks for his agreeing to meet. I handed James the tobacco I used to acknowledge Frank's gift, and we sat for a moment in silence. Then James spoke.

"We see things happen," he said, "but don't take the time to understand. You have. You and your friends have been blessed."

Rather than continue to comment on my experience, James felt called upon to share his own. This was unusual. The Lakota way is still closely held. But James was now speaking to me as another soul who had touched the same source. He spoke of his initiation as a healer and his work with the community.

"I wish all Lakota could hear the Eagle talking to them in their language." Then he paused, "If everyone heard the voice of the Creator in their own language, the world would be a happier place."

James talked about William Powers, whom he knew of growing up on the Rosebud Reservation in Pine Ridge, South Dakota. He confirmed what Powers wrote. But it was an entirely different experience hearing James speak the same Lakota words, and feel the energy behind them, rather than seeing them on a page. Our meeting was coming to a close. James lifted the tobacco from the table and placed it in his down jacket. Then we said our goodbyes.

The following Monday I was back at work, but my meeting with James was still fresh in my mind: The cry of an eagle. The flight of a hawk. And yes, the ping of a marble. Most of us would not allow the possibility that these are different ways of saying the same thing. But to find their equivalence is to see beyond the shape of their expression, and discover the wondrous moment when spirit connects with matter. It is also the intersection where "I" becomes "Thou." There's no need to journey to ancient ruins, remote mountaintops, or magical lakes shrouded in lore to find these mystical moments. If you listen, they will find you, when and where you least expect it: in laundry rooms, bedrooms, busses, backyards, basements, vegetable gardens, roadsides, and crawl spaces. The humdrum is as much

Thoreau's "distant drummer," as the common clover is a lotus flower.

Geraldo was not a colleague I regularly chatted with, but for some reason I felt drawn to his office when I returned from Minnesota. Up to this point, we had never shared anything of a personal nature. When we met, it was all business. I was sure he didn't know anything about Frank's marbles.

I should also mention that in all this time I had never actually posed the question, "Did you happen to find a marble recently?" to anyone. I knew it would sound not only odd, but preposterous. And what's more, I had no reason to fish for miracles when they seemed to be biting everywhere. I had enough on my hands. So I kept the story among a few friends and trusted colleagues, and that was all.

Geraldo, however, was the first and only person to whom I ever felt inclined to "pop" the question. And I did, gingerly. And I will never forget his reaction.

"Geraldo," I said, in a tone as matter-of-fact as could be, "did you by chance happen to come across a marble anytime since late August, perhaps while digging, or something of that nature?

My question was met with stunned silence.

"Why?" he asked.

I looked at him and sensed his astonishment.

"Why are you asking me that?" Geraldo suddenly seemed defensive.

"I don't know," I said. "I just thought I'd ask. I'm writing about some events that happened over the summer and it occurred to me that something similar may have happened to you."

"What? What happened?"

His agitation was growing. I could see tears welling in his eyes. Clearly my question had a resounding effect. But I did not want to color his perspective in any way.

"Why don't you tell me your story first," I said, "And then I'll share mine."

"Okay," Geraldo agreed. "But you have to promise you'll tell me."

"Of course," I said.

Geraldo breathed a sigh and sat back in his chair.

"You have to understand," he said. "I haven't told anyone. Not even my wife. It's like..." He paused in mid-sentence, still contemplating whether to proceed.

"Like what?" I asked.

"It's like you know my deepest secret."

Geraldo had my attention now. I assured him it was okay. That he could share his secret.

"It was a Sunday afternoon in late August," he continued. "I was standing in the back of my yard. I can't say I was very happy."

"What was going on?" I inquired.

"For one thing I'd been out of work for a number of months. And Nina, my wife, was also laid off at the same time. On top of that, we just moved into our new house with our two daughters."

"That had to be scary," I said, "being out of work."

"Yes, but it wasn't just our financial position that made me anxious. I was feeling discouraged, totally unrecognized. I was praying all the time. I was calling out to God and getting no response."

"And what happened?" I prompted.

"My house in Central New Jersey was built on a wooded, undeveloped parcel of land. The backyard is too rocky to plant anything. So after Mass on Sunday I usually spent an hour or two digging up rocks and depositing them in the woods. That Sunday I was digging out rocks and uncovered a dusty blue marble."

"A marble?" I asked, containing my excitement.

"Yes, a marble. At first I wondered how it got there. And how long ago. It didn't seem possible that it could be in the spot where I found it. Then I thought of my childhood in Havana, Cuba. We didn't have expensive toys. We played with marbles. The marble transported me to memories I hadn't visited in years. It was a marvelous time. It was a clear message, a sweet message. A healing answer to my prayers. I know it sounds strange. But from then on, I knew everything was going to be okay."

"What did you do with the marble?" I asked.

"I felt uncomfortable sharing the discovery with my wife. I figured she'd think I was nuts or something. So I went inside the house and placed the marble inside a small wooden box, a special box, adorned with carvings, and inlayed with mother of pearl. The box was a gift from a dear friend."

Not surprisingly, I was floored.

I was the person who hired Geraldo, and thereby fulfilled the prophecy he gleaned from his blue marble, that everything was going to be okay. That he would be recognized. That he would find employment, restoring his financial stability. Similarly, Geraldo offered further validation of the over-arching marble-related events in a story that was reminiscent of the one Miles had recently shared with me in Minnesota. It was my turn to floor Geraldo, the second time that morning.

I told him about Frank and all the events that had transpired since his death. We were each brought to tears by the other's story and our deep sense of recognition. The next thing I knew we were standing in the middle of Geraldo's office, hugging, practically crying, like long-lost brothers who have stumbled on each other.

I will admit to being a little dismayed that Geraldo lifted his gift of hope from the ground and kept his revelation in a box. That he felt it was too big a secret to share with his wife. Then again, I could understand how vesting an object with so much spiritual energy could rouse some envy from a spouse, who, I should add, had just returned home with Geraldo from church, an institution in which marbles are not specifically sanctified.

Not surprisingly, however, much as in the Vedic tradition, there is in Christianity, as there is in Sufism, evidence of game playing, of sacredness as divine sport.

I read that in 16th century Spain, John of the Cross' favorite game was playing "hide and seek" with God. "God's games," he called it. Fortunately, the Inquisition didn't take issue with his fun. Or with another of his ideas, comparing souls to stones buried in the earth. Where did John of the Cross get that idea? In his time, there was opposition to monks engaging in manual labor. But that didn't stop John from doing what he enjoyed, working as a mason and a carpenter. For all we know, while digging the foundation for the monastery he designed at Granada, he could have found a small stone or marble just like Frank's. Or perhaps John picked up a cue from the Old Testament. *Adam* is the Hebrew word for man. Derived from *adamah*, it means ground or soil, the substance into which God breathed life, creating humankind and all the animals.

Within the Judeo-Christian tradition, however, it is the words of Jan Van Ruysbroek, a 14th century Flemish monk, that leave me amazed. He writes in *The Sparkling Stone,* of a small, smooth, "wholly round" stone that brings forth an Eternal Light, teaches us Divine Truth, and fills the world with love. "Yet none can attain It," he says, because, "It reveals Itself where It wills and when It wills." For Ruysbroek, the stone is Christ himself.

But let us return to our time. Nearly one hundred years after confirmation of Einstein's Relativity Theory, we still have the expectation that life should fit neatly into little square boxes, that we arrange sequentially on a calendar, that we think is separated in time from places on maps. But that is all a convenient fiction. There is unassailable evidence at the quantum level for what is called non-locality, meaning constituents of matter are not space-time dependent. When objects that are separated in space-time act in concert, they are called entrained. But what about much larger chunks of matter...like marbles? Can they display entrainment? My question is, "Why not?"

Take, as an example, the collective marble finds of Frank, Miles, Geraldo, and Don—all strangers to each other.

Miles digs up two marbles in Minnesota that stir

recollections of his marble-playing days on a Lakota Reservation in the late forties. Geraldo digs up a marble in his backyard in New Jersey that stirs memories of his marble-playing days in Havana, Cuba, in the late fifties. Frank unearths his marble in an old cistern in a crawl space under my house in Pennsylvania. Don digs up a marble in Minnesota that winds up in the hands of Gwen. Their discoveries span thousands of miles and are weeks and months apart. Nevertheless, they each marvel at their discovery, which, for Miles (who lost his cousin) and Geraldo (who lost his job), immediately elicits a sense of peace at a distressing moment in their lives.

How do our typical calendar/clock notions of time explain this confluence of events? Defying time and space, what connects them? What is the principle at work? In a sense, they are entrained. That is how I see it. And if so, something outside the sphere of time and the laws of cause and effect must be operating. Carl Jung called these phenomena synchronistic. Meaning is the glue that connects such events. But for me, there still remains another vital force in the equation: marble = miracle. And that, of course, is Frank, who must also be operating beyond space-time to coordinate such an impressive show.

It was now six months since Frank's death and a few days into the New Year. I was nearing completion of this book, or so I thought. In actuality I wasn't even close. For one thing, marble discoveries were occurring regularly and not just on Sundays. I could hardly keep up with them. More than once I would get an excited call in the night. The one that stands out most was from Ryan, a friend and attorney who, among other things, advised me on how to legally restrain Björn, Anne's crazy ex, except now it was Ryan who needed to exercise some restraint.

"Who are you?" Ryan was yelling at me on the phone. "Some kind of fucking prophet?"

I'd never heard him sound angry before.

"What's going on?"

"I found a crystal marble this evening."

"How 'bout that," I said. "What happened?"

"I needed to pick up some work and I saw it, scattering light on the path to my office."

"Seriously," he continued. "This is ridiculous."

"How so?" I asked.

"I don't know. It just is." And he hung up.

Ryan was a successful attorney who launched his career at the U.S. Department of Justice, working on the landmark antitrust case against AT&T. Advertising firms and start-up telecom companies throughout the U.S. could thank Ryan for assisting in the break-up of that monopoly and opening the door to competition.

Still, when Ryan's own monolithic worldview was tested, he wasn't pleased. He came face to face with a larger reality, almost tripping over the evidence. He even picked it up and held it in his hands: a multifaceted crystal marble or stone. Instead of feeling awed, he got angry. As rich and successful as he was, Ryan was not King of this Reality—the Reality that allows a marble to drop in from nowhere, proving nowhere is everywhere. Ryan could perform some impressive legal maneuvers. However, spiritual maneuvers beyond his control obviously left him angry and dumbfounded.

I don't mean to judge my friend. I was saddened

by his behavior. Two years later Ryan killed himself. A neighbor found him hanging in his garage. He was in the middle of a divorce and his practice was in decline. But surely if his viewpoint was not so fixed, if he had chosen love over anger and could release some of his cynicism, he might be alive today. The way I see it, Frank tossed Ryan a lifeboat in the form of a marble: a new way to look at himself and the world. But Ryan would not accept it.

Frank tossed me the same lifeboat. I was now ready to jump in. I was tired of the constraints of my job. I could see where it was all heading. There is loose in our world a spirit-crushing machine that is choking a Voice we desperately need to listen to. And that Voice includes our own. Everything is being commoditized, systematically stamped with an insipid sameness. I decided there was one thing I wasn't going to allow the machine to crush: a stubborn little marble that rolled into my life; a gift from Frank that pointed the way back to my soul. It was time to take my chances and see where it would take me. It was time to deliver my resignation to Richard.

CHAPTER 9

I shall play the game of my undoing.
— Tagore

And so it is February of 2004, late afternoon, six months after Frank's death. I remain under the spell of a common playing marble, a child's trinket. But it is not just any marble, of course. It is how it appeared, the meaning that clings to it, the fact that more keep turning up, and the timing of their appearance. Together it adds up to a message of great import.

No event has so consumed my attention. Even meeting Anne, the woman I loved, and love itself, does not possess the power to intrigue me as much as this round sphere of glass. I feel it calling me, challenging me. Surely, this is mad. I don't have much money saved up. No trust fund. No golden parachute. And the truth is I am over-qualified for the kinds of freelance projects that are likely to sprout up. Remember, the spirit-crushing machine demands sameness. It doesn't need me.

I pace my office, weighing these thoughts, holding my resignation letter, as the soft winter light filters through my window, offering no view of the future; only the faintest shadow of an unbounded world into which I know I must cross. I sign the letter and stroll into Richard's suite across the hall. He sees me standing by the door. He's on the phone and signals me to come in.

Again, we're sitting across each other, separated by his big desk. I don't mean to eavesdrop, but I hear him speaking to his wife, preparing for their family trip to Jamaica. It must be nice, I thought, to call a travel agent and have everything taken care of. Frank's my travel agent. And all he sent me was a marble. Thanks Frank!

"How is everything?" Richard asks.

"Very good," I respond. "Everything's good." But he can see I'm fidgeting with a folded letter in my hand.

"How's Anne? That ex of hers still giving you guys a hard time?"

"Fortunately, that's behind us."

"Excellent. I'm glad to hear it."

"Richard," I said, "I decided it's time for me to move on," handing him my resignation letter.

"Really?" he asks. "Are you taking another position?"

"No," I said. "It's nothing like that."

"And you're sure about this?"

"I've given it a lot of thought," I said. "I think it's the best thing for me right now. You know about the marbles from Frank?"

Richard nods.

"Leah found some, too," I said, in a lame attempt to bolster my argument.

"Yes, she mentioned it to me."

"Well, I decided to write a book about it. "

"A book?"

"Yes. And I feel like I need some time to explore it."

Richard chuckled a bit, but in a delighted sort of way. After all, what do you say to a key employee who is leaving because of a marble? On the other hand, when you are sitting in the owner's seat, I'm not sure it matters all that much whether one employee stays or leaves. You can always hire another.

"How are you going to manage, financially?"

"I have a little money saved up."

"I'll tell you what. Go ahead and work on the EIS account. I'm sure they can use your help. That'll be some income."

"What about my non-compete?" I asked.

"Don't worry about it."

"Thank you," I said.

Usually when a manager leaves a company he is forbidden to work on any agency business for at least a year. Richard's offer was a godsend. I knew the client liked me and I would have some work to keep me going. I had taken a leap of faith. And now, at least, there was a little padding at the landing.

"You'll give us a couple of weeks?" We were in the middle of trying to win another piece of business.

"Of course," I said, "whatever you need."

We shook hands and gave each other a big hug.

I left Richard's office a free man. But that's not to say I didn't have any obligations, or that the future was going to be easy.

Teresa came running up to me as I was leaving Richard's office.

"You're not going to believe this," she said.

"On the contrary," I smiled back, "I probably will."

"My mom's dog, Buddy, led her to a marble!"

Teresa was a young art director I had recently been working with on a project. During that time she shared with me a running debate she was having with her mother, Betty.

Betty saw herself as a passionate Aquarian. "There is much more to life than we know," she'd say, trying to convince Teresa.

"I'm a rational Capricorn," Teresa would counter. "I need to see something to believe it's true."

I told Teresa she should listen to her mom. And then I told her about Frank and all the marbles people were finding.

"C'mon, you're kidding, right? That's just weird."

"I know, but it's true," I said.

And then I made a startling prediction. "You know, Teresa, your mom's going to find a marble too."

Teresa gave me a look of disbelief, "If anyone is going to find one, it would be her."

"Well, I'm still skeptical," she insisted, when she shared the news of her mom's marble find.

"So you told your mom about the marbles before Buddy led her to one?" I inquired, like any diligent reporter.

"Yes, I told her before. But I'm sure she wouldn't make this stuff up. Who could?"

"Exactly," I said. "That's the point. Who could?"

Teresa smiled. "I'll think about that."

"Would it be okay if I spoke with your mom?"

"Sure," Teresa said, pausing to jot down her number. "I'm sure she'd love it."

As a dog lover, it was Frank's customary habit to approach every New York City pooch with a big, affable, "Hi, Buddy!" So when Teresa told me there was a dog named "Buddy" behind her mother's discovery, I knew it had Frank's imprint. I called Betty right away from my office.

Here's how she told it:

"I have a small, white Maltese dog, Buddy, who is eight years old. Buddy was diagnosed with Cushing's disease, a people disease, where the adrenal glands pump extra cortisone into the brain. As a result, Buddy feels hungry and thirsty all the time. Every night when I go to bed, Buddy gets a pill. I keep Fruit Gems in the drawer of my night table so I can stuff his pill in the candy. Last night I opened the drawer and right next to the candy was a clear marble with a light blue oval inside. When I saw it, my heart skipped a beat. There wasn't a marble there the night before, or any night before. It came from nowhere."

"Perhaps it happened so Teresa would find something greater to believe in," Betty added, waiting for my response.

"Well," I spoke honestly, "if that's the case, I don't think it moved Teresa off the dime."

"Yes," Betty agreed. "That's my daughter."

In the 1930s, with the advent of Quantum Field Theory, physicist Abraham Pais declared an "end to the game of marbles." I would respectfully submit that thanks to Frank Bava it has been reformulated to fit a world grounded in information. And so the game is not over. Not by any stretch.

I thought it was a good time to check in with Luz, the nurse's assistant who helped Frank look after his mother, and with whom he fell in love, to learn if Frank had ever communicated anything to her about the marble he carried around.

"Yes," she said when I called. "Frank showed it to me after his mother died. We were in her bedroom, boxing some things for a local charity. He told me how he found it and what it meant to him. How much peace it brought him."

"Did you think that was strange?" I asked.

"Who has not picked up a small stone at one time and felt something special? Someone might laugh. People laugh at things they don't understand."

I invite the reader to consider the men and women of science and the laboratories in which they work. Theirs are funded by governments and major institutions, filled with expensive, finely machined devices, laid out in complex arrays to catch nature in its most hidden, private moments. Such experiments cost millions, if not billions, of dollars. Exploding atoms into smaller and smaller pieces, looking for smaller and smaller things, is an expensive enterprise.

In contrast, consider my laboratory, which I presume is not much different from yours with respect to its contents. No special equipment, just the stuff of life. Everyday objects—like tables and chairs. Does that make my laboratory or yours any less valid as a place from which to observe the world? As John C. Lilly noted, "Science is imbedded in practically every human activity." In other words, you can practice science anywhere.

The biggest criticism of experiments like the one I hastily set up with Frank is that the results cannot be duplicated. My response is, "Why not?" I am not suggesting everyone deposit a special or prized object in the suit of a dearly departed friend or loved one and expect to get it back the next day. Or that your neighbor will find it, too. And your neighbor's neighbor. What I am suggesting, however, is that simply by observing your own thoughts and intentions and what's going on around you, the results I observed may be duplicated, and therefore conclusive for those individuals who feel repetition spells truth. What happens when we examine nature in this manner? Nature smiles back.

"That's crazy," the scientist says. "A smile is no more than a facial reflex. And in this case a mere projection on your part. Nature doesn't smile."

"And that, Sir," I would say, "is simply because you have been making it cry for too long."

Nature wants to play. But if it is abused, subdued, or neglected for too long, the dam will burst. Like one's soul, it demands recognition, or it will strike back, bringing sickness, neurosis, depression, or despair.

News of my resignation was rolling through the agency. I still owed Richard two more weeks of service. Honoring that, I shifted my focus back to work. Or rather, tried. There was a soft knock outside my office. I looked up. It was Marty, an account manager.

"Can we talk a second?"

"Sure," I said, "have a seat. And if you want any furniture from my office, now's a good time to claim it."

Marty laughed. "Yeah, I heard. Wow, you're really cutting out? And business is good right now."

"I know. It makes it harder. Walking out at a good time."

"Well, best of luck to you."

"Thank you," I said. I stood up and we shook hands.

"I've been meaning to ask you something. About the marbles…"

"You heard about them?"

"C'mon Michael, who hasn't? It's pretty amazing."

Marty sat down and revealed an emotional side that I hadn't seen before.

"When my father died suddenly a couple of years ago, I was distraught," he confided. "So my wife Linda told me I should seek counsel with our rabbi."

"Did that help?" I asked.

"Not very much. He isn't the most *hamish* of men, if you know what I mean."

"Actually, I do. My mother spoke Yiddish. In other words, his bedside manner left something to be desired."

"Exactly. Rather than engage in any kind of

discussion, the rabbi referred me to a book. Very thoughtful, huh? I wasn't looking for a reading list. Anyway, I read it, and I can't say it brought me much comfort."

I could see Marty was getting teary.

"So how can I help?" I asked.

"A few months ago, I was installing a medicine cabinet with my son as part of a bathroom renovation. I needed to check for level. But instead of using a small mechanical level, which of course is the right tool for the job, something impelled me to ask my son for a marble."

"'Don't you want a level, Dad?' My son looked at me like I wasn't all there."

"'No,'" I said. "'See if you can find a marble.' So my son came back with a clear marble, with a lime green swirl. Keep in mind that I hadn't heard a thing about your marble, or anyone else's. I placed the marble inside the cabinet and saw that it didn't roll. And that's how I checked to make sure the cabinet was square."

"That seems pretty clever," I said.

"I suppose so. But here's the thing. Once the job was done, I felt inexplicably attached to the marble. And I didn't give it back to my son. I placed it in a small jewelry case, where I knew I wouldn't lose it. And I felt how proud my father would have been about the renovation, since we did stuff like that together all the time."

"Could it be," Marty wanted to know, "that my dad was with me the day I asked my son for a marble?"

"Of that you can be sure," I told Marty, handing him a box of Kleenex I had near my desk. "He'll always be with you."

"Thanks, man" he said. "We'll miss you around here."

We've all chuckled at cartoons where, in one scene, a dog is running from a man, and in the next the man is running from the dog. Back and forth, the pursuer becoming the pursued. In the end, we can't really say who is who. I was feeling the same way. I wasn't sure if I was the dog or the man. The more I tried to chase down the story, the more the story chased me. In hope of solving this dilemma, science puts a glass between itself and the experiment. On one side is the observer in his white lab coat, on the other, the object of study. But everyone knows, or *should* know, that it is a charade. The glass is a prop. It does not guarantee objectivity. It only obscures the lack of it. It allows the observer to maintain the illusion of independence. In truth, the one who sees, and the object that is being seen, are both intimately bound with the other. Like it or not, we not only are in this together, we *are* this together.

Joanne was a friend of Frank's and a salon owner in New York where Frank once worked. She had a dream about him shortly after he died. In her dream, Frank was fixing a pipe under her bathroom sink. She thought he was applying some kind of magical remedy, as if he were trying to fix it with a wink and prayer. When she walked into the bathroom, he turned and smiled. Her dream ended with Frank's unforgettable grin.

Months later, in the early morning hours on a Sunday before Christmas, Joanne noticed a leak in her bathroom. She opened the cabinet under the sink to find a leaking pipe. When she reached for a bucket to collect the water, she noticed a clear marble in a basket of cleaning supplies. There was no good explanation for how it got there. Then she recalled her dream, and Frank's smile.

"It's nice to have a marble from Frank," Joanne told me. "But I didn't feel the need for one. I already got a demonstration."

"What do you mean?" I asked.

"On the day I heard about Frank's death, I was working at my computer. When I opened the application to launch a directory of many hundreds of names, the file had mysteriously disappeared. Instead, it read, 'only one record.' And that one record was 'Frank Bava.' Then Frank's name began flashing on my screen."

"Wow, that must have stopped you."

"It did. I was so startled I shrieked. I couldn't shut down my computer fast enough. And when I re-started it a few minutes later, the application worked as usual. All the records were back."

"What did you make of that?"

"You know Frank. He was having a laugh. He was always making fun of my incessant problems with electronics. He was playing around, making his presence known over the very medium we used to joke about."

During my last few days at the office, I did not detect any insincerity from my colleagues for the reason I resigned. Unless they were pulling my leg, humoring a "Mad Finder" of marble treasures in their midst, I'd felt the consensus was, "Yes, this is important. It is worth examining." Then again, we were all working in the same business. Surely they had to admire this message from the Absolute. And I don't mean Vodka.

The EIS account Richard offered up, despite the non-compete clause, would channel me some work. With that promise in hand, and some parting words to my friends, I got in my car and shifted my thoughts to the road ahead. Within a few months, more marbles came rolling into my life with the same rhythmic intensity. Just when I caught up with my writing, a new discovery would be revealed. And every one seemed perfectly timed to keep me engaged. Frank was no Pavlov. He would not for a moment allow me to extinguish the expectation of the miraculous.

With the first anniversary of Frank's death, I'd felt another spiral had begun. I happened to look up at the weeping cherry tree near my house from the same spot where Jean had stood during the weekend we spent together. The tent moths were back. The circle had come around. I was looking back on that moment as I took the same steps to rid the tree of these insects. But without Frank's help, the challenge became a chore. I missed my friend. Anne and I were still seeing each other. And I resolved to visit Frank's resting place at Calverton as soon as we could.

As the months progressed, and my days of corporate toil were largely replaced by the writing of this book, many people who had already discovered a marble were blessed with another one. Gigi's second marble, for example, arrived special delivery in Florida. And this time she was there to receive it.

As before, a man strolled into the store and walked around.

"He was thin," Gigi said. "He had sweet eyes and a warm smile. There was a simple beauty about him that was very pleasant."

According to Gigi, he was wearing an old beige shirt and a worn Fedora. "He gave the impression of someone who worked outside, close to the earth," She said. "There was dirt around his fingernails and in the creases of his long hands."

"I have something for you," he told Gigi, reaching into his pocket. "It's important for me to give this to you," he said, placing one marble gently in her hand. Then he reached into his pocket again and disclosed a handful of marbles. "Every time I give one of these away, it helps me." And that was all he revealed.

"I understand," Gigi said, smiling, awed at the beautiful marbles he held out to her. A hundred questions raced through her mind, but before she could proffer any, a customer distracted her, and the man slipped away.

"Frank always wore old beige coveralls when we worked," I told Gigi. "Beige was his color."

Leah's marbles kept coming, too.

On the morning of Sunday, September 19, 2004, the weather turned cold in Princeton, and Leah went in search of a sweater for her daughter, Jennifer, who was being baptized that afternoon. Leah's search took her into the basement where she had recently organized some storage boxes. She was shocked to find a solid green marble near her furnace, almost a year to the day when she stepped on a round green stone in her bedroom. Leah could offer no practical explanation for it. But now she allowed it to touch her heart.

"This time I could accept the stone for what it was," she admitted to me, "a gift from God."

Leah was enormously grateful for her child's good health, as well as her own, having in the past year gone through heart surgery, followed by a difficult pregnancy.

But in addition to Leah's discovery that morning, something else quite unexpected occurred that afternoon. The priest who was presiding over her daughter's baptism picked the wrong moment to pour water over Jennifer's face. For an infant, the sprinkling of holy water came as a deluge. Suddenly, Jennifer was drowning. As her daughter's face turned white—"as white as her dress," Leah said—she had the presence of mind to pick Jennifer up and slap her on her back. Jennifer started breathing again. It was a frightening moment, to say the least. Poor Jennifer, I thought, way too young to be placed physically on the razor's edge between torture and benediction; and poor Leah, who had to witness it.

As Leah was telling me this story she brought up Frank, and how he died in a pool in Queens. I hadn't considered it that way, that Frank's death was a kind of baptism. But I had to agree that in his passing he created an opportunity for us to embrace a much larger dimension by making it visible, by reaching out across the veils of space and time and thereby revealing the shabbiness of our commonly held notions, and why our obstinacy in accepting greater truths is often an expression of fear.

Perhaps in the course of your travels, when you feel close to the limit of what your heart or soul can endure, you may come across a small stone or marble quietly resting on the ground beside you, or on the chair next to you, or even hand-delivered by a saintly presence. Surprised, you may wonder, "Is God reaching out to me?"

Gloria, a woman who knew Frank, called me to say she found a beach ball on her front lawn. "It looks like a marble," she said, trying to sound happy about it.

"A beach ball is as good as a marble," I told her, trying to cheer her up. "It's *all* a marble. We're *on* a marble. We call it earth."

"I don't understand," Gloria said. "How could everything be a marble?"

"Try substituting the word miracle for marble, and you'll see my point." I could sense Gloria wrapping her mind around this.

"So everything is... a miracle?"

"Correct. Every minute. Every second. Without miracles nothing would exist. When you are feeling down, that simple thought, everything is a miracle, will change everything. Trust me. If that wasn't true, how could it change anything?"

"I don't know about that," Gloria said. "But I'll try it."

The truth is I was feeling sorry for Gloria, because she knew Frank and felt left out. So I decided to break convention (funny how the miraculous had become conventional) and simply purchase one for her. Until then, I always let Frank make the decision. After all, isn't that what makes it miraculous, that the marble *finds* the person? I felt odd about it, as if I was cheating, and vowed this would be the first and only time I would break precedent. Shopping around, I found an old clay marble from the 1800's in a nearby antique mall.

When I inquired about it, the attendant remarked, "That's pretty. Is it for you?"

"No," I said. "It's a gift for a friend."

Nearly fourteen months later, on election night 2004, I was waiting in line to vote. I found myself standing in front of a volunteer election official for the township. We looked at each other. She smiled in a friendly way and seemed vaguely familiar.

"Do we know each other?" I asked.

We continued to look at each other. Keep in mind, this was in the midst of a noisy crowd, waiting, as I was, to exercise their civic duty and leave as soon as possible.

Then her face lit up and she screamed, "The marble!"

I was shocked, of course. It was an exclamation that crossed party lines. Suddenly, everyone was looking at us.

Then the woman called her husband, excitedly. "Dave, this is the man who bought the marble!" Her voice rising again.

Dave didn't have the slightest idea what his wife was talking about when we shook hands and said hello.

Linda, the election coordinator, was the same woman at the antique mall who sold me the marble I purchased as a gift for Gloria fourteen months before. Imagine, in the intervening time, how many hundreds of items and heirlooms of far greater monetary value Linda would have sold. But, for some reason inexplicable to her, she vividly remembered that particular sale. "Why?"

"I don't know," she said. "I just sensed something special about it."

Linda has an impressive voice. And she wasn't shy about using it. The marble I purchased for Gloria led to a kind of resounding cry of "Gloria in excelsis Deo" in a school gym packed on election night. At least that's how I heard it when Linda screamed, "The Marble!" Her cry was one more piercing sign. I don't think of myself as anything special. But I understand the madness of martyrs.

Stan Tenen is an independent scholar in Jewish philosophy who also has a degree in physics. Through an examination of the letter sequences in the Book of Genesis, he discovered a surprising link between the geometry of its letterforms and human gesture.

In *The Alphabet That Changed the World*, a book layered with profound significance, Tenen shows how every moment and every manifestation is infused with a generative process that begins with the Grace of God. "The coin and currency of God's Love," Tenen writes in an article titled "A Personal God," is *shefa tal*, translated as 'effulgence of dew.'" *Tal* is the seed of emergent phenomena, one bit of God's love, one unit of information, one particle of radiant dew, as if God were blowing soap bubbles into our earthly dimension from an infinite and timeless expanse. *Tal*, as an "expression of singularity," contributes to our understanding of how God can be perceived as the Many and the One, as personally relevant, and wholly objective. *Tal*, as Tenen sees it, is an invitation to transform our humanity

to achieve new levels of social harmony. *Tal* is Stan
Tenen's marble, and like the pinging noises I heard in
the clothes dryer when Frank's marble was signaling its
presence, the *Bet-Bet-Bet* of *Tal* "rains on every pool in
every field in heaven and on earth."

There are many stories of mourners who in their
grief cannot accept death. In a dream, perhaps, or in
a reverie, the deceased makes himself known. The
mourner feels comforted by this presence, perhaps felt
as the soft touch on a shoulder, or a wisp of a scent, or
even a familiar song that suddenly plays on the radio.
Is this wishful thinking? Some psychologists tell us
death is our only fear; anything else, rather, everything
else, is a pale reflection. They say that our minds create
phantoms and signs of lost loved ones, and any patterns
or coincidences we find and attribute to them is simply
magical thinking to insulate us from the harsh reality
of death.

Perhaps there will be individuals who will look
upon what has been told here as one enormous collective and unconscious effort to deny the painful experience of death, or a dear friend's passing. But can this
really account for the revelations of those for whom
Frank was as anonymous as the name of the salon
where he worked. Engaged in the business of life, we
had little time to conjure up signs and symbols out of
the ether to fill the gap left by his passing.

Anne Brener, in a beautiful book called *Mourning
and Mitzvah*, says of departing souls that they have a
direct link to God. "Is there a message you would want
to send up with the soul of the deceased?" she asks.
"Perhaps a prayer for your own healing?" Then she

suggests putting the request in writing, and offering it up to the soul you are mourning, so that it may be "carried to higher realms."

I think there is something in our makeup that recognizes the timing and technique to facilitate this communication. When I read Brener's suggestion, I recalled my own impromptu message to Frank: "Toss it back if you're ever around." And I thought of Joanne, too.

Joanne called me just before the New Year to tell me about a celebration she held Christmas Eve. Like me, she wasn't familiar with Brener's book, but she conceived a similar strategy. To each of her friends and family members she handed one marble, and invited them to make a wish for themselves, and say a prayer for Frank or a loved one. Then she collected the marbles and placed them in a silk pouch.

"But I don't know what to do with all the marbles," she said.

"Let's take them to Frank next Sunday in Calverton," I suggested, adding, "he'll know what to do."

I phoned Paula and invited her to join us. Her father is also buried at Calverton and, coincidentally, the anniversary of his death was the night I called.

The three of us planned to make the trip to Frank's resting place within a few weeks. But a winter storm delayed our plans. Then personal and professional commitments intervened. And as the months passed, our schedules were never able to line up. That's when I decided to make the trip myself. I told Anne, and she offered to join me. We agreed to go as soon as we could get away.

On a late Sunday afternoon in early October,

Anne and I drove to Frank's grave in Calverton. It was a year and two months since Frank's death. We stood silently among rows of white markers all meticulously aligned. Anne lightly kissed the ground beneath which Frank rested and laid some daisies by his headstone. It was a spot of yellow, in addition to the setting sun, in a sea of green and white.

Frank used to wear a St. Christopher medal, the patron saint of travelers, around his neck. And now, with his death, he has himself become an Hermes-like agent, inviting us to discover a greater soul within, and infinite intelligence throughout. That Hermes, the Greek god of transitions and boundaries, was also identified with Thoth, the Egyptian god of healing and the inventor of writing, is no surprise to me. The writing of this book has been my healing. And if you have come with me this far, perhaps it has contributed to your own.

CHAPTER 10

A handful of dust could hide your signal...
Now that I am wiser
I read it in all that hid it before.

— Tagore

In all my research, one comment rose above the rest. It is from a book on the philosophy of religion titled *Time and Eternity* by W. T. Stace. He says, "If owning a marble leaves your metaphysical and religious thirst unquenched, so will owning all the planets."

Stace was making a point about scale, that it's insignificant. That with regard to the material world, one marble, one planet, one anything is essentially the same as another. In today's parlance, it's just information. The more joyful truth is discovering what's beneath appearances, not getting caught up in them.

Naturally, I agree with Stace, who penned his orb-laden thought in Princeton, six decades down the road from where I had worked the corporate shift. But a far more compelling coincidence was when I learned that for nearly thirty years, a research team at Princeton University was also playing with marbles, thousands of them. They were observing, if not miracles, something tantalizingly close. Soon we would have the pleasure of meeting and comparing notes. How about that—Frank and me, welcomed in the hallowed halls of science. But I am getting away from myself. I will cover that ground soon enough.

At this moment, I've been at the marble game for nearly a decade. I have put my faith in the message that the marble carries. I recognize my confusion when I began, that I was caught between two worlds: the one we consensually agree is real, with fast-food restaurants and dry cleaners; and the greater one of which everything is a part. The catch, of course, occurs when the greater lets you know It's there, and the unwritten contract that sustains the former is sharply repealed. Until then, it's pretty much status quo. After that, anything goes. Of course, I don't mean that as license to do anything. On the contrary, ethical behavior becomes more imperative when the connections become more apparent.

I suppose, in hindsight, I could have outsourced the task of my own spiritual evolution to a Teacher or Guru, like one would go to a financial adviser to manage their savings. I could have plunked my marble down on my Teacher's meditation cushion and asked, "How should I invest it?" On the other hand, I am not sure it's a good practice to outsource one's being, unless it is directly to the Source Itself.

By now I have developed a kind of uncanny sense for when a marble will appear, or when I can expect to hear about some discovery, or even when and where to rendezvous, as if I was a secret courier picking up a clandestine message.

Usually a marble arrives at a moment when I need some encouragement, some reassurance that I should continue my labors, not worry about the debt that I have accumulated writing this story, living on a handful of projects that have come my way in a tough economy. "Keep going," I tell myself. Or better yet, as Meher Baba, Avatar and Marble Aficionado put it, "Don't worry. Be happy."

I was thinking about all this one rainy Sunday afternoon when I needed a break from wrestling with a language that knows only subjects and objects, that resists a world in which they are the same, thereby imprisoning our minds in an artificial framework. On that rainy afternoon something pointed my car to a flea market where there was little likelihood of any vendors showing up because of the weather. But there was one, his stuff displayed on a grey, rickety table of wrinkled wood. A spark of light hit me from a little cardboard box. I looked closer. It was a marble made of quartz, just like Frank's.

Sure, it's a flea market. You'd expect to find a marble. Nothing special, right? I inquire about it. The vendor looks at me, completely surprised. "Wow!" he exclaims, looking at the stone. "How'd that get there?" And then he adds. "Take it. It's free. It must be for you."

"Thank you," I said. And as I wave good-bye, I continue to hear him uttering his dismay at the unaccounted item in his inventory.

There have been many incredible marble discoveries. And they continue. I trust, however, that I have placed before the reader enough evidence to make my points, and perhaps reaffirm some timeless truths. That the soul never dies. That nature is in constant communication with us. That the universe will play lovingly and lightly with us if we approach It in the same spirit. That we are energetically knitted to the subtle fabric of everything we touch via our minds and bodies, though habit and predispositions do not allow us to see it. That however deeply we are hurt, God will help us heal if we allow it. And that we must endeavor to respect these truths, not under the illusion that it will make everything easy, but that we will be more at peace if we do.

The reader may wonder why it's taken so long to write these words. At just around 140 pages, I have managed to produce on average about 14 pages a year. That surely is not a very impressive output.

The truth is I find narrative writing a miserable grind. English is the language of commerce and cultural domination. It is a blunt instrument when it comes to matters of the heart. Then, too, I am as inertia-bound and comfort-oriented as the next person. I'm happy to grab a beer and binge on Netflix for hours, even days. I once watched the entire series of *Breaking Bad*, getting up only to use the bathroom or drop a slice of pizza in the oven. That's because it is infinitely more difficult to live breaking good. Why we are wired that way, I don't know. But it is a fact. To change the trajectory of one's life when we are unhappy or not living our truth is no easy feat.

One day in the spring of 2013 I suffered the consequences of this neglect. I was cycling with two friends on a Sunday afternoon. I turned sharply to avoid a pothole and slammed into the ground, fracturing my hip. It was a mean and painful crash. I was rushed to hospital and had surgery the next day.

My femur was cracked at the head in a couple of places. The ball of the femur that slides in the pelvis, the marble, if you will, was separated from the bone. I was helpless and in terrible pain. I was smote, hip and thigh. And this metaphor was instantly apparent to me. I was squandering my time. I was not honoring Frank's gift. "Complete the book," was the message. "I will hobble you until it is done." So I buckled down. Rather, I should say, knuckled down, though I could hardly bend down to tie my shoes. I dusted off the manuscript and let something greater guide my pen.

Where was Anne, the love of my life, during this painful time? She called a few months after our trip to Frank's grave to say she was getting married: A successful salesman with an attractive crop of black hair… who looked like Steve Young…the former quarterback of the San Francisco 49ers. Then she called back a few years later to tell me they had separated. Yes, she admitted, she had made another bad decision. "And how are the marbles?" she added. I'm embarrassed to say I gave us another chance. But briefly. As in *Gone With The Wind*, I'd finally had enough of playing Rhett Butler to Anne's Scarlet, of her Pavlovian knack for extinguishing my ability to care.

We live on shifting sands and take little notice until the foundation cracks. The friend that loves you today will find fault with you tomorrow. The boss that praises your work will look for someone to do it for less. The people you once nurtured or supported will be too occupied to help when you could use a hand yourself. And all through life, with the exception, perhaps, of a tiny few, people will make the mistake of seeing you as something you are not. And you, from your own bias, will do the same to them. The only thing you can count on is the dialogue you maintain with yourself and with God. Everything else is a distraction. If you can keep that straight, as a healthy tree grows strong and balanced over the ball of its root, indeed, its marble, you will do well. "Standing up straight continuously in whatever circumstances we are in"—this is what it means to be "fearless," Dainin Katagiri, a Japanese Zen master, tells us, and to be open to what is "omnipresent."

I have come to see the stones and marbles that many of us cherish, store in special holders, carry in our pockets, or wear close to our hearts as emblems of the self. The Greater Self. The mani-jewel. In Sanskrit, the *cintamani*, the fabulous gem that answers every wish. It is the core we seek but can never quite enter. We can only bask in its manifold reflection, and be thankful for the moments of pure consciousness and love that it offers, before it revolves again, revealing aspects of ourselves that we may not comprehend, but must find the courage to face.

What began as a marble tucked in a eulogy delivered to a dear friend has transformed itself as a testament to life and to healing and the deeply inspiring beauty of a world that will work in concert with us if we simply allow it, raising miracles to the surface of our lives. May you one day be so fortunate as to experience ever so profound a truth from a simple bead of glass.

EPILOGUE: 9,000 MARBLES

"**M**arbles have mystical qualities." The calm authority in which Bob Jahn says this surprises me. "Indeed," he continues, "they are magical."

Bob isn't a spokesman for the toy industry, trying to resurrect a game that has long been supplanted by more sophisticated technology. Bob was a rocket scientist who worked on propulsion systems with NASA, a Professor of Aerospace Sciences and Dean Emeritus of Princeton University's School of Engineering and Applied Science. He was also the founder and director of the Princeton Engineering Anomalies Research, or PEAR, laboratory that functioned in the engineering school from 1979 until 2007. Today, he is Chairman of International Consciousness Research Laboratories

(ICRL). Along with Brenda Dunne, the President of ICRL and Bob's long-time writing and research partner, we are sitting in Brenda's office at their headquarters in Princeton, NJ. It is early March of 2014.

What is gratifying for me about this meeting is that Bob and Brenda will validate every step of my journey with respect to the implications of today's science in light of their own pioneering research in human consciousness.

But the meeting is also tinged with irony, when I realize that all the years I've been trudging through the thicket, they've been constructing a logical path through a similar landscape, only a few miles away. They didn't hear me bushwhacking, and I didn't have their map. Neither did I yet have the pleasure of speaking with Jack Engstrom, who heads an organization founded by Arthur Young called The Institute for the Study of Consciousness. Jack has devoted much of his life to exploring the ontological ground excavated by Arthur Young, and framed by G. Spencer-Brown in *Laws of Form*. Jack introduced me to Bob and Brenda's first book, *Margins of Reality*, just as I was completing mine. I enjoyed it immensely. So when I learned they lived in Princeton, I called to introduce myself. And we agreed to meet as soon as convenient.

Do I need their validation? No. The proof of this story is my truth. But is it nice to have? Yes. Because skeptics abound despite ample evidence for the extraordinary interactions that occur between mind and matter; between *many* minds and matter; and between matter and minds such as Frank's, that has shed its physical profile. As Bob and Brenda explain it, my good friend can now be described as "An infinite wave function that demonstrates frequency and amplitude without the constraints of time." Nonetheless, he will always be Frank to those of us who loved him.

Not the least of PEAR's proof of the impact of human consciousness on "objective" reality comes from an extraordinary apparatus that contains 9,000 marbles! Or, to be more precise, 8,999 marbles, since Bob and Brenda graciously offered me one, a gift I happily accepted, with a bit of trepidation that one less might skew their studies.

Here is how their great marble apparatus works: 9,000 finely machined marbles made of a composite material, randomly trickle down from the top of the device through an elaborate array of 330 pegs, and come to rest in 1 of 19 bins, each equipped with a sensor that counts the marbles. In an unaided run, to establish benchmarks as free as possible from user influence, the terminal pattern of the marbles will reflect a random distribution when they collect at the bottom. Now, add a human subject into the room, who is directed to sit a few feet from the device, and who is allowed the intention of informing the process, and something incredible happens. The results deviate from the control, proving the effect of consciousness. This has been demonstrated time and again. Using this machine and other devices that generate random binary data, Bob and Brenda have amassed a boatload of evidence that shows the impact of human consciousness on the environment.

Curiously, the same statistical evidence used to ground more accepted principles in science, like quantum theory, is condemned when it comes to demonstrating the influence of mind in nature. Many in the scientific community, even the institution that once hosted them, are not enamored of Bob and Brenda's work. That begs the question, "What are they so afraid of?" Remember Galileo, who faced the Inquisition because he had the courage to present irrefutable proof that the earth revolves around the sun? The Catholic Church ultimately apologized to Galileo. But it took 350 years.

Nothing is so powerful, or as vulnerable, as Truth.

The statistics of large numbers tell us why it is possible, even likely, for one person to win the lottery twice. For the winner, it feels like a miracle. For the statistician, it's just another day at the office. It stands to reason that if more people are looking for marbles, the likelihood is more people will find them. But what about situations where people *aren't* looking for marbles? And marbles are finding them through an Agency that displays consciousness, intelligence, and compassion, indeed, all the hallmarks of a prior incarnation in human form? This is the distinction that challenges us to look at the world in a new way. Perhaps we are approaching a threshold when our society will accept this reality, not atavistically, but as something that will lead us to a more evolved state.

Skeptics will gather the usual arguments. But there will be a few among them who will find a marble and wonder, "How did that get here?" I know such people. I was one of them. They may go as far as to admit that what looks like a miracle is simply a mystery that awaits explanation. Indeed, throughout history, that has often been the case. If so, all this may amount to a drunkard's dream, which, in any event, we know to be true, for such deception is wired into how we see the world.

I send love and prayers to my friend, Frank Bava, and to everyone who is not afraid to question the Authorized Version when they sense a deeper truth beneath the surface.

SOURCES

I am indebted to Hans Christian von Baeyer's book, *Information: The New Language of Science*, published by Harvard University Press in 2003. While Frank's marble qua information is solely my interpretation, this book ignited the spark from which the idea grew. It also provided a vital bridge to other concepts that von Baeyer wonderfully elucidates, including the work of Claude Shannon, the weakness of Shannon's theory in solving the question of meaning, and John Archibald Wheeler's contribution to Information Theory.

The quote at the start of Chapter 2 comes from *Pilgrim at Tinker Creek* by Annie Dillard, published in 1972 by HarperCollins. I was amused to learn that when Dillard was a child she would hide pennies in little roadside nooks, and by the roots of trees. I suppose it's likely that Frank impersonators may one day do the same with marbles. Werner R. Loewenstein's quote in Chapter 2 comes from his book, *Physics in Mind: A Quantum View of the Brain*, published by Basics Books.

The quote at the beginning of Chapter 3 is from a book entitled *Sarmad The Saint* by Dr. M.G. Gupta, published in India by M.G. Publishers. Rumi's quote that starts Chapter 4 is from a book entitled *Open Secrets, Versions of Rumi,* by Coleman Barks and John Moynes, published by Threshold Books. In Chapter 7 the attributions to Henry Horace Williams are from *The Evolution of Logic,* published by the author in 1925. G. Spencer-Brown sources include: the first British edition of his book, *Laws of Form,* published by George Allen and Unwin Ltd; his work of prose, *Only Two Can Play This Game,* which, published by Bantam in 1972, he wrote as James Keys; and, an excellent transcript of Spencer-Brown's presentation at Esalen Institute in 1973, which can be found at lawsofform.org. I learned much about Abraham, the patriarch, from David Klinghoffer's book, *The Discovery of God,* published by Doubleday in 2003.

Rabindranath Tagore's quotes at the start of Chapter 9, and Chapter 10, are from *Fruit-Gathering,* first published in 1916. The marble-playing references to Meher Baba were gleaned from meherbabatheavatar.org. Printed in 1993, Anne Brener's book is entitled *Mourning & Mitzvah 2nd Edition: A Guided Journal for Walking the Mourner's Path Through Grief to Healing.* Permission granted by Jewish Lights Publishing, Woodstock, VT, www.jewishlights.com.

In Chapter 10, the declaration of an end to the game of marbles is from a book by Abraham Pais entitled *Inward Bound,* published by Oxford University Press. The quotes from Dainin Katagiri in Chapter 10 are from his book, *Returning to Silence, Zen Practice in Daily Life,* published by Shambhala Dragon Editions.

ACKNOWLEDGEMENTS

Let me thank all the finders of marbles and spherical treasures who graciously shared their stories in a universe that continues to respond to our playful and prayerful dialogue. Among this group special thanks go to Jean Harvey, Gretl Glagget, Glenda Gracia, Lyle Iron Moccasin, Beryl Katz, Joni Johnson, Miguel and Raysa Ferry. With thanks, also, to Richard Gillespie, who observed the beginnings of this story with humor and compassion as I fell under the marble spell. During the months following my cycling injury, I would not have survived without my dear friend Patrice Scully, who helped elevate both the work and me, and who also provided additional editorial assistance as this work neared completion. With respect to that period, much appreciation also goes to Chuck Carpenter, a supremely talented Rolfer. I want to thank Joan Guccione for her warmth and for keeping my fledging finances going while writing this book. For our many enjoyable discussions over matters numinous, many thanks to Jason Hutchinson. Heartfelt thanks also go to friends and readers who offered insight and encouragement, including Suda and Mark Handleman, Neil Melker, Noah Lambert; and, for their editorial insight, Jean Harvey, Mary Lou Hutchinson, and from ICRL Press, Mary Bonanno and Patrick Huyghe. A big thank you goes to Stephen Larmer for his work on the cover art. I want to acknowledge Laura Jacobus, a loving friend and an extraordinary woman, whose thoughts helped refine this book, and who conveyed, in many wonderful ways, the presence of Frank, confirming for me in her gift of a thangka, Frank's emanation as an enlightened being. For their friendship, their scholarship, the clarity and patience in which they transmit the dharma, much love and appreciation goes to Joshua and Diana Cutler of the Tibetan Buddhist Learning Center. I want to express my thanks to Stan and Levanah Tenen of the Meru Foundation for taking me inside their "tent" and sharing an exciting new way to look at the world. Theirs is one of the more amazing books I have ever read. I want to say *tashi deley* to Rinchen Dharlo for the kindness and blessings he has extended to me over the years. And express my appreciation to Jack Engstrom for his generous insight, his vibrant and lucid thinking, and for introducing me to the work of Brenda Dunne and Bob Jahn. To Brenda and Bob, who know a miracle when they see one, a special note of gratitude for their suggestions, and for publishing this book. Lastly, I want to acknowledge two special people I have come to love with all my heart, Steven and Susan, my brother and sister. While we grew up terribly isolated, today we stand together, only occasionally looking back at the great chasm we have crossed. Thank you all for making this book far better than it would be without you, and the world a better place for everyone.